中國夢・廣東故事
——活力的廣東

作者　徐靜 XU JING

The China Dream :
Guangdong Story - Dynamism

Editors: Lu Xuehua, Wu Mingxin

Published by Guangdong People's Publishing House Ltd.,

China www.gdpph.com

First published 2017

Printed in the People's Republic of China

The China Dream: Guangdong Story-Dynamism/ Xu Jing and translated by Liu Xiaoxue

ISBN 978-7-218-11890-1 (paperback, 1st edition)

Preface

Located in southern China, Guangdong Province is the first region in China to implement the reform and opening up, and it is also one of the most affluent areas nationwide. The Pearl River, China's third largest river, runs across the whole province. The Pearl River Delta is an alluvial plain flushed by the Pearl River. After nearly 40 years of rapid development, it has already become one of the most important city groups of China. The Hong Kong Special Administrative Region, and the Macao Special Administrative Region adjoin to Guangdong Province. With the natural geographical relations and the same cultural background, they constitute China's unique Guangdong-Hong Kong-Macao Greater Bay Area—a world-class vigorous economic and cultural area.

For nearly 40 years of rapid development, Guangdong has been playing a leading role in innovation, spurring the rapid development of new growth drivers. There are many rapidly grown-up enterprises in Guangdong, such as Huawei, Tencent, and UMi, which have become important engines of Guangdong's new economy development. Huawei and Tencent are now widely known in China. We try to approach such enterprises and their employees, to find the "secret" of the most innovative and cutting-edge development in Guangdong.

Guangdong has been the most dynamic foreign trade area in China since ancient times. And Guangzhou has been a commercial city through the ages, as well as an important interconnecting city alongside the "Maritime Silk Road". Foreigners from all over the world travel across major cities in Guangdong everyday, sightseeing, attending business meetings, studying or visiting friends. In Guangzhou, there are a large number of foreigners from Europe, America, Southeast Asia, the Middle East, Africa and other places, doing business here everyday. They ship back clothing, fabric, seafood, electrical appliances or glasses; foreign trade is booming. In the Shenzhen Special Economic Zone ports, people and vehicles travelling between Hong Kong and Shenzhen are always lined up. Foreigners living here for many years gradually adopt and merge into customs and culture of Guangdong, and regard Guangdong as their "second home". Meanwhile, tens of millions of workers from other provinces live in Guangdong, especially in the Pearl River Delta, where they work in factories, earn money to support their families, and try to realize their own dreams and ambitions. Whether foreigners or migrant workers, they are all practitioners, promoters and witnesses of Guangdong's reform and opening up. We conduct close observation of their work and life to record their ups and downs.

Ten years ago, the per capita income in the Pearl River Delta had already reached the level of that of moderately developed countries, and it is moving towards high-income phase. But the embarrassment is that in the eastern, western and northern parts of Guangdong Province, there are still large number of underdeveloped rural areas, and some places are even in extreme poverty, which distresses successive provincial governments. The government is determined to carry out large-scale " poverty alleviation" action, and vows to lift all peasants of impoverished areas out of poverty in three years, and promote common prosperity in these parts of Guangdong like the Pearl River Delta.

As the most populated, dynamic, and developed province that has been spearheading reform and opening up, recent practices in Guangdong are full of strength and sweetness. We go into it, and hope to find and record those breathtaking, touching and impressive stories of the development in Guangdong these years. Those people and those stories constitute a glaring part in the glittering development of the new era in Guangdong.

Through these stories, you can see diligence and endeavors of Guangdong people in the process of modernization. Through the perspective of Guangdong, you can see great efforts of Chinese people in realizing the China dream of the great rejuvenation of the Chinese nation.

　　廣東省位於中國南部，是中國最早實行改革開放的區域，也是目前中國最富庶的地區之一。中國的第三大河流珠江穿越廣東省全境，由珠江沖積而成的珠江三角洲在經過近四十年迅速發展後，已經成為中國最重要的城市群之一。香港特別行政區、澳門特別行政區與廣東省毗鄰，天然的地緣和一脈相承的人文情緣，構成了中國獨有的粵港澳大灣區──一個世界級活躍的經濟人文區域。

　　和中國其他地區一樣，在經過長達近四十年的高速發展之後，廣東面臨產業轉型升級轉變發展動能的重任，創新驅動成為推動此輪變革的重要抓手。廣東省內有許多近年來快速成長起來的新型企業，比如華為、騰訊、有米科技，它們成為廣東新經濟發展的重要引擎。華為和騰訊，以及它們的「老闆」任正非和馬化騰，在中國幾乎家喻戶曉。我們試圖走近這樣的企業及其員工，找到廣東創新驅動最前沿的發展「密碼」。

　　廣東自古以來是中國對外商貿最活躍的地區，廣州是千年商都，是「海上絲綢之路」重要的節點城市。來自世界各地的外國人每天往來於廣東省內各大城市，他們或旅遊觀光，或商務會議，或求學訪友。在廣州，每天大量來自歐美、東南亞、中東和非洲等地的外國人在這裡做生意，他們把這裡的服裝、布匹、海產品、電器或者眼鏡託運回國，外貿做得紅紅火火。在深圳經濟特區口岸，進出香港和深圳的車輛、人流常常排成長龍。長年生活在這裡的外國人，在生活習俗和文化上逐漸接受並慢慢融入廣東，廣東成為他們的「第二故鄉」。與此同時，更多的數千萬計的來自中國內地的普通勞工常年生活在廣東尤其是珠江三角洲地區，他們在工廠裡「打工」，憑藉「打工」掙下的錢養家餬口，並試圖實現自己的人生夢想。無論是外國人還是農民工，他們都是廣東改革開放的實踐者、推動者和見證者。我們近距離觀察他們的工作和生活，記錄他們的喜怒哀樂。

珠江三角洲地區早在十年前人均收入便已達到中等發達國家水平，正邁向高收入階段。但令人尷尬的是，在廣東省的東、西、北部仍有大片生活並不富裕的農村，一些地方甚至還處於貧困狀態，這讓廣東省歷屆政府頗感頭痛。政府下決心開展大規模的「扶貧」行動，並發誓要在三年後讓所有貧困地區的農民擺脫貧困，力促粵東西北地區與珠江三角洲地區走向共同富裕。

作為人口最多、經濟最活躍、總量最大、地處改革開放前沿的省份，廣東近年的實踐既具有力量又讓人感到溫馨。我們深入其中，希望通過我們去發現去記錄，在廣東發展這些年中，那些或動人心魄或充滿溫情或飽含人性的故事。那些人，那些事，終將構成廣東新時期史詩般發展歷程中炫目的一環。

通過這些故事，人們可以看見，在現代化進程中廣東人的奮發圖景；透過廣東，可以看見中國人民為實現中華民族偉大復興的中國夢的奮鬥歷程。

Jiangmen: Still a Door to Sea

江門：依舊海之門

Guangzhou:
The Ancient Port
Achieves New
Developments

The Past and Present of Huangpu Ancient Port

In December 2015, Guangzhou, the provincial capital of Guangdong province, a metropolis with more than 13 million population, was holding the "Goteborg" porcelain exhibition in Guangzhou Museum. The nearly 100 pieces of porcelain set out from Guangzhou in 1745 but slept more than 200 years at the seabed of the Swedish port of Goteborg. In the words of the Chinese people, it is regarded as "back home".

On January 11, 1745, the Swedish merchant ship "Goteborg" went back home from Guangzhou. The ship was loaded with about 700 tons of Chinese goods purchased in Guangzhou, including 366 tons of tea, 500,000 to 700,000 porcelains, as well as silk, rattan articles and mother of pearl. It is the third time this ship came to Guangzhou, also the last time.

In 1757, the Qing government announced the implementation of "Canton System". The countries traded with China all needed to and could only come to Guangzhou.

That year, according to China's old calendar, was the 22nd year of Qianlong in Qing Dynasty. Qianlong was the reign-title of the imperator Aisin Giorro Hongli at that time. In ancient China, when the new emperor ascended the throne, a reign-title was set to calculate years to distinguish from the predecessor (mostly his own father). The 22nd year of Qianlong has been the year when Qianlong was on the throne for 22 years.

Qianlong means "Blessed Prosper and Flourishment", and the fact is the case. Qianlong, with a life span of 88 years, was the emperor who lived the longest in ancient China. The period, from his grandfather Emperor Kangxi (one of the ancient imperators who were most appreciated by Chinese) to his father Emperor Yongzheng to Emperor Qianlong, was the heyday of culture, economy and handicraft industry in

▲ "Kang-Qian Flourishing Age", in which "Qian" refers to the Emperor Qianlong, is in Chinese history the heyday of culture, economy and handicraft industry. The picture shows the Emperor Qianlong.

Chinese history. In China, the greatest praise for a dynasty is named as flourishing age— maintaining prosperity in a long time—the three emperors created China's "Kang-Qian Flouring Age".

"Qian" in " Kang-Qian Flourishing Age" represents Emperor Qianlong. Qianlong claimed to be "The Shi Quan Old Man", with "Shi Quan" meaning perfect, from which the emperor's self-confidence is obviously seen. In China, he was also the one who wrote the largest number of ancient poems which were said to be more than 30,000, and even those great poets in the golden age of Tang Poem and Song Verse cannot be compared with him.

After 35 years' implementation of " Canton System", in 1792, Britain sent the fleet of Macartney to China in the name of making up for celebrating Qianlong's 80th birthday. According to the rules, vassal states needed to kneel when they saw the emperor. The two sides had controversies over whether to kneel or not and how to kneel on the matter of dignity and state system but in fact more of cultural gap. Later generations will hold the view that it is a symbol of China's change from openness to seclusion.

After sailing for 8 months, the "Goteborg" came to the sea about 900 meters away from the Port of Goteborg, and the crews who had been 30 months away from home could see their hometown. However, at that time, the bow hit the rocks and immediately sank. People who were waiting for triumphant return on the shore had to watch the ship sailing to the sea. Fortunately, all the crew were safe and sound.

About one-third of the goods were salvaged. These goods were sold on the market and unexpectedly made a profit of 14 percent in addition to pay the full cost of the trip to Guangzhou. The ship "Goteborg" and two- third of the goods were buried at the bottom of the sea, quietly waiting for the moment more than 200 years later to once more see the light of day.

In 1984, a Swedish folk archeological activity found the wreckage of the ship "Goteborg". Two years later, archaeological excavations began.

▲ "Goteborg III" visited Guangzhou.

Soon, more than 400 pieces of complete porcelain and 9 tons of porcelain pieces were salvaged. Most of these porcelains were with traditional Chinese patterns, and a small amount of porcelains were painted with characteristic European patterns. Obviously, they were specially ordered by "Goteborg specially" for specific customers.

150 years later, in 2009, the " Goteborg" once again came to Guangzhou. However, this time it was a new ship built by imitation of the old ship. Chinese people habitually call it "Goteborg III".

It took craftsmen ten years and cost 30 million US dollars to build this ship.

To welcome the "new friends", Guangzhou spent a huge sum of money reconstructing two wharfs at Huangpu Ancient Port and Nanhai

God Temple. The two piers and their surroundings are modeled on the ancient style, restoring the scene more than 200 years ago. They want to show Chinese marine culture represented by the maritime Silk Road, Guangzhou's history of trade, and reshape the reputation of the ancient port in the world.

The sailing route of "Goteborg III" was also arranged in accordance with the sailing route of "Goteborg", which is the longest sailing route in the world before the 16th century. Everything went well, but it spent more than 300 days coming to Guangzhou with a journey of 3700 km.

The Swedish king, Carl XVI Gustaf, and the Queen Sylvia arrived on the same ship. It is said that it is the king's own request to select Guangzhou as the first destination in China. Cantonese lived up to Swedish people's friendship, and visitors streamed into Guangzhou.

The new-sharp magazine *New Weekly* made a comment on this trip: two cities in two countries, with an archaistic sailing ship and an ancient business routes, performed a wonderful show with 200 years of historical connotations. CCTV recorded this pioneering work into the "Discovery" column, and Cantonese saw it as "an unaffordable great opportunity to promote Guangzhou". The Swedish turned the plan into a very creative "cultural image project". The renascence of "Goteborg"shows successful public relations, including marketing of sponsors, international trades and cultural exchanges.

"Goteborg III" is connected to the history and future of Guangzhou's foreign contacts. After arriving Guangzhou, as in 1857, it parked in

Huangpu Ancient Port—a port which had never lost contact with the outside world for 1500 years and the only port which allowed for trading when the Seclusion Policy was carried out in the late Qing Dynasty.

"All foreign merchant ships importing foreign goods shall not berth along the river bay and must be anchored in Huangpu." Huangpu is Huangpu Ancient Port. Within the 80 years from 1758 to 1837, there were 5107 foreign merchant ships parking in the ancient port of Huangpu. As the only port in China for a long period, it witnessed the prosperity of "Maritime Silk Road" in Guangzhou. It also welcomed the U.S. merchant ship "Empress of China", the Russian "Hope" and other foreign merchant

▲ The Memorial Archway of Huangpu Ancient Port.

ships, especially the "Empress of China" whose visit to China opened the door of Sino-US trade.

The Chinese historian Huang Renyu pointed out in his book *A Year of No Significance* from a historical point of view that China's

falling behind in the process of modernization was not due to moral and personal factors but the technological failure in achieving "mathematical management." But in some figures, in fact, Chinese people have done well. For example, about the statistics of the 5107 ships.

▲ That year merchant ships gathered on the Pearl River.

The great Chinese historian, litterateur and ideologist Sima Qian once wrote that Guangzhou is a metropolis "full of pearls, hawksbills, fruits and fabrics". Huangpu Ancient Port is located at Xingang East Road in Haizhu District in Guangzhou. Huangpu Village, where Huang Port locates in, keeps still the quaint scenery with a large banyan tree next to the ferry standing askew, shining banana trees and few fishing boats, without any traces of business.

The original name of Huangpu Village is "Fengpu". In the south of

the village there stands a colorful memorial archway with two characters "Feng" and "Pu" on it near the Pearl River. As a legend goes, a pair of Phoenix flied into this place, after which the population increased and people had a bumper grain harvest. Legend will always be beautiful and auspicious.

The village locates in a small island. In China, the waterside area is called "Pu", and the land in water is "Zhou". So the village is named "Huangzhou" or "Fengpu", and then its name developed into "Huangpu".

A lot of historical sites and cultural relics kept by the village witness generational prosperities of the "Ancient Maritime Silk Road", prove the unique historical status of Huangpu Ancient Port, and reflect the great changes taking place in Guangzhou. Huangpu village is a living museum of "Ancient Maritime Silk Road", because the most valuable history exists in the hearts of people.

The prosperous development of Huangpu Ancient Port is in the 17th century to the 19th century when the development of the overseas trade in Guangzhou comes to its peak, that is, "the golden age of trade to China" which is what the modern Western businessmen often talks about. In 1769 the British man William Hick came to Guangzhou. He was full of praise for Guangzhou: "The scene of ships running on the Pearl River is like the Thames under London Bridge, and the differences between them lie in the different forms sailing boats on the river as well as galleons." In the eyes of foreigners, nothing is more spectacular than the long array of sailing ships.

Some people made an evaluation like this: ships set sail from Huangpu Ancient Port in Guangzhou in the east seacoast, transport silk, porcelain, and tea to all parts of the world. At the same time, farming and handicraft technology, papermaking technology and compass were also taken to them. Monks, scientists, artists and translators who took the merchant ships back and forth are the messengers promoting cultural integration. In this sense, in the long history of thousands of years, as one of the birthplaces of the maritime Silk Road, Guangzhou is a starting point of the trip for Chinese

▲ Huangpu Ancient Port.

civilization to have an influence on the world.

The old days have gone. The glory of the past gradually disappears in the gradually silted ferry of ancient port. And the pier is not busy and bustling as it was. History should be borne in mind. It is not a bad idea to build a historical museum of Huangpu Ancient Port, and Cantonese have done so.

One ancestral hall in the village is reconstructed into the historical museum of Huangpu Ancient Port. The area of 2000 square meters consists of three parts: the mural area, the area of material object and the central area. Among them, the area of material object is the most distinctive part of the museum. Designers gathered together more than 40 pieces of ancient building materials scattered in the ancient village of Huangpu, such as stone beams, stone pillars, stone carvings to create a scenic area of "Ruins" in the yard. They did not enclose these cultural relics to show them to visitors, because they hoped visitors could closely feel the glory of the culture of the ancient port.

In the mural area of the exhibition hall, there lies a large gilded mural made of white marble, with 31 meters in length and 15 meters in height. The painting portrays the prosperous scene of thousands of ships in Huangpu Ancient Port during the period when the "Canton System" was implemented. "Goteborg" and "Empress of China" are among them. This mural should be designed based on pictures left by some foreigners when they made sketches.

In Huangpu Ancient Port, an important seaport for foreign trade, many ships gather, economy prospers and the villagers also have early contact with foreigners and foreign cultures. Many villagers study abroad, engage in trade and become celebrities. For example, Hu Xuanze, the consul of Qing government, Japan and Russia in Singapore; Liang Cheng, the student who studied in America and reclaimed extra indemnities from the American president to construct Tsinghua University; Feng Zhaoxian, the one who delayed his disease for rescuing Sun Yat-sen, as well as the rail expert Hu Dongchao, the agricultural expert Feng Rui and the economist Liang Fangzhong.

In the Huangpu Village, there is a mysterious story about a Japanese wife who protects villagers from Japanese army invasion, which is quite legendary.

In 1900, Feng Zuoping, a villager in Huangpu Village, studied in Japan and met a Japanese girl. They soon got married. In 1924, because of homesickness and the need to attend upon parents, Feng Zuoping who was more than 40 years old came back to Huangpu Village from Japan with his families.

In order to release his wife's homesickness, Feng Zuoping built a small Japanese-style house for his wife, so that she could live in peace. This is the "Japanese House" now located at No.8, Dunyong Street in Huangpu Village.

After Japan launched the war of aggression, Guangzhou was occupied. A team of Japanese troops came to the Huangpu Village , and the villagers would soon be slaughtered. Suddenly, Feng Zuoping's wife appeared in front of the Japanese, showing a treasured sword. After Japanese troops saw the sword, they put their swords down, venerably worship the treasured sword, and then went out of the village. During the Anti-Japanese War, the Japanese army never invaded the village of Huangpu.

Villagers near the village got to know that the Japanese troops did not dare to enter Huangpu Village, they had to hide in the village of Huangpu. Therefore, Huangpu Village is also known as "Ping'an Village", with "Ping'an" meaning "safe". In 1944, Feng Zuoping's wife died of illness and was buried on the top of the mountain inside Huangpu Village.

About the origin of the knife, in Huangpu Village there are three kinds of popular sayings. The first saying is that Feng Zuoping's wife is a remote relative of the Emperor of Japan. It is also said that she is a general's niece at the end of Japanese Shogunate period, and the sword is given by the general; one more saying is that she is a prime minister's niece, and the sword is given by the prime minister.

An old man who is familiar with the history of the village is more in favor of the third saying. "Japan is a hierarchical country. If she is from the royal family or the shogun's relative, she is impossible to marry an alien or a civilian." Anyhow, the Japanese wife makes great contributions to Huangpu Village.

Maintain Prosperous
for 2000 Years

"Goteborg" did not make it when it would come home soon after going through difficulties. However, "Nanhai No.1", another ship which Chinese people are more familiar with, soon sank into the sea after leaving Quanzhou Port in China.

Quanzhou, another important port in ancient China, is one of the four major ports in the world in Tang Dynasty, the largest port in Song Dynasty and labelled by Marco Polo as "the Bright City". Marco Polo may be one of the few Italians who are more famous in China than in Italy. He described his experience in China in *The Travels of Marco Polo*, which aroused Europeans' enthusiastic longing for the Orient, and had a tremendous impact on the future discovery of new travel routes. However, many people doubt that his descriptions of China are sometimes slightly exaggerated.

Different from "Goteborg" which can only be imaged by future generations, "Nanhai No.1" who witnesses the history of Maritime Silk Road can show us his true appearance because of the complete evacuation. In 1987, in Yangjiang, a sea area in the southern province of Guangdong, a shipwreck with a history of 800 years was found. It was later known as "Nanhai No.1" and is by far, among all discovered shipwrecks, the oldest, largest and most complete merchant ship for ocean trade in the world. It is estimated that it is 30.4 meters long, 9.8 meters wide, and the hull (not including the mast) is about 4 meters high. The displacement is more than 600 tons, and the dead weight capacity is about 800 tons. In fact, we do not know the name of this ship. Perhaps it has no name.

After "Nanhai No.1" was loaded at Quanzhou Port, probably due to storm or leak or some other unknown reasons, it finally sank into the sea. Exactly 20 years later, it was found and salvaged by creatively employing the plan of "raising integrally". The shipwrecks and cultural relics together with their surrounding water and silt were hoisted and transferred to the museum of "Maritime Silk Road" in Guangdong province, and then these cultural relics were sorted.

No one does not care about what is in the "Nanhai No.1". On January 15, 2016, a total of more than 14,000 sets of cultural relics and 2575 specimens were unearthed, among which there were more than 13,000 pieces of porcelain, 151 sets of gold, 124 sets of silver, 170 pieces of

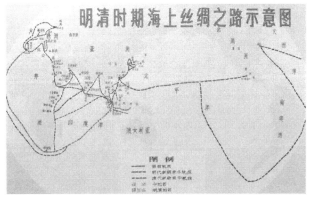

▲ The Maritime Silk Road in the Ming and Qing Dynasties.

bronze, about 17,000 coins and lots of animal and plant specimens, ship wood and so on.

"Nanhai No.1" is on the channel of the ancient Maritime Silk Road. Maritime Silk Road is the main artery of marine traffic connecting the East and West. Because the main bulk commodities are silk, it is named "Maritime Silk Road". As the goods transported changes, it has also been called "the maritime road of ceramics" and "the maritime road of spices". Starting from the southeast coast of China, through the Indochina Peninsula, the South China Sea countries and then the Indian Ocean, getting into the Red Sea, the ship arrived in East Africa and Europe. In the Song and Yuan Dynasties, China had a direct business contact through "Maritime Silk Road" with more than 60 countries in the world. The success of Zheng He's voyage in the Ming Dynasty indicated that Maritime Silk Road developed to its heyday.

Despite the prosperity, during quite a long period the Maritime Silk Road is only found in few documentary records, so people know little about it. Until in the 20th century when porcelain, silk and other cultural relics from China were found one after another at the ports along the route, Maritime Silk Road were gradually known to us. "Nanhai No.1" can provide a credible model for the study of this phase of history, and even restore and fill a historical gap related to it, and even more presents the information documents and land archaeology cannot provide.

Within Chinese territory, Maritime Silk Road mainly consists of three main ports including Guangzhou, Quanzhou and Ningbo as well as feeder ports including Yangzhou, Fuzhou and others. Since the 230s, Guangzhou has been the main port of Maritime Silk Road. It is known as only major port with enduring prosperity for more than 2000 years in the history of marine traffic in the world.

In 2015, China officially established "The Belt and Road" strategy (abbreviated as B&R) which is the abbreviation of the Silk Road Economic Belt and the 21st-Century Maritime Silk Road. It would fully rely on the existing double multilateral mechanism between China and relevant countries, with the existing and effective regional cooperation platform, borrow historical symbols of the ancient Silk Road, hold high the banner of peaceful development, actively develop economic partnership with the countries along the line, and create an interest community of political mutual trust, economic integration and cultural tolerance, a community with a common future and a community with common responsibility.

Guangzhou's "Stretching" Exercises

In the 19th century, the Sino-US trade was realized through transactions between commercial firms. There was a businessman named Wu Bingjian, whose firm had long enjoyed a good reputation in the United States and whose business almost monopolized the market. However, compared with his real name, the merchant Howqua was more well-known to American businessmen, and Hu-Kwa Tea is hence the name.

In 2014, Robert Forbes, the associate professor of the University of Connecticut and the director of the Forbes Museum, established the Forbes House Museum, the first Sino-American trade museum, in his ancestral home left by his ancestors in Milton, Boston. This museum, whose area is small, well preserved every item brought back by his ancestors from Guangzhou.

Robert Forbes' great-great-grandfather is also named Robert Forbes. At the age of 13, with all kinds of hardships, he came to Guangzhou by a merchant ship and went to his uncle who ran a firm to learn doing business. He kept close contact with Wu Bingjian. When he left Guangzhou, Wu Bingjian gave him a self-portrait as a souvenir. It is in the process of listening to these past events, looking at these carefully preserved Chinese portraits and porcelain that Robert Forbes slowly grows up.

Wu Bingjian's father, Wu Guoying, had been engaged in foreign trade and set up the Ewo Hong in 1783. Wu Bingjian was born in 1769. At the age of 32, he took over the Ewo Hong, after which his family business grows up rapidly. At the age of 60, he and his family owned the property up to 26 million silver dollars. They not only owned real estate, house property, tea mountains, shops and huge sums of money in China, but also invested in railways, securities trading and insurance business in the United States. The Ewo Hong became a veritable multinational consortium.

In 2001, the Wall Street Journal specifically made a list of the world's richest 50 people in the last 1000 years. Among them, there are six Chinese people, including Genghis Khan, Kublai Khan, Liu Jin, He Shen, Wu Bingjian and Tseven Soong. The Wall Street Journal made a comment like this. "Born in 1769, the Qing Dynasty Merchants Wu Bingjian, inherited his father's business, engaged in foreign trade, and further lent foreign merchants money and hereby obtained great

▲ The businessman Wu Bingjian in Qing Dynasty enjoyed a great popularity in the western business circles.

wealth. He enjoyed a great popularity in the Western commercial circles."

Western businessmen considered Wu Bingjian to be "honest, cordial, careful, generous, and rich", and the British complimented him for his skill in financial management and extremely intelligence. It is said that Wu Bingjian adopted advanced business philosophy and established a close contact with important customers in Europe and the United States. As a widespread story goes, an American businessman was unable to pay off his debts of more than $ 70,000 to Wu Bingjian due to poor management. After Wu Bingjun learned of it, he tore up the receipt and announced the accounts were settled, so that the businessman could return to his home. Wu Bingjian knew well the importance of the "trademark". He attached his portrait to the tea sold overseas. Although this seemingly thin businessman did not leave Guangzhou throughout his life, his portrait went to the Americas, Britain and India with the goods.

▲ The trade in the Thirteen-Trades Monopoly in the Late Qing Dynasty in the 18th century.

▲ Zhujiang New Town, the CBD of Guangzhou city, is a symbol of the rapid development of Guangzhou. In the picture the two tallest buildings are respectively Guangzhou International Finance Centre and Chow Tai Fook Finance Centre (on the right). Below the picture is Haixinsha, the place where the opening ceremony of Guangzhou Asian Games was held, a small island in the Pearl River. Photographer: Liu Lei

The great businessman in the late Qing dynasty was once the richest man in the Thirteen-Trades Monopoly, and the Ewo Hong has also become the epitome of the development of the Thirteen-Trades Monopoly. The Thirteen-Trades Monopoly is the general term of the foreign-trade firms specially permitted by the government, not necessarily thirteen firms.

After the " Canton System" was carried out in Guangzhou, businessmen from the Thirteen-Trades Monopoly became the only housekeepers dealing with foreign affairs of the Qing Dynasty during more than 80 years. In addition to doing business, for foreign businessmen, things like sales of goods and their daily routines, whether important or trivial, must be handled by the Thirteen-Trades Monopoly.

However, after Treaty of Nanking provided for the opening of Guangzhou, Xiamen, Fuzhou, Ningbo and Shanghai as treaty ports (known as the "five-port trading"), the Thirteen-Trades Monopoly no longer had the exclusive monopoly of China's foreign trade. And the Thirteen- Trades Monopoly was declining.

The Thirteen-Trades Monopoly was once the commercial center of Guangzhou. The vicinity of the place where it is located, including the Beijing Road area has always been the administrative center of Guangzhou city, the center of Cantonese culture in modern China and the most prosperous commercial distribution center in the history of Guangzhou.

Until after the policy of reform and opening-up was implemented, the business district in the central old city area with the Beijing Road shopping district as the core and the business district along the central axes of the new city area with the Teemall as the core, became the dual power motivating the development of Guangzhou city and its economy together.

Guangzhou changes so fast. The change of city centers, from the city landmark, Nanfang Building, with a saying "One who fails to reach Nanfang Building does not actually come to Guangzhou", to the later Beijing Road Pedestrian Street, Tianhe Teemall and the present Zhujiang New Town, has witnessed the development of Guangzhou city. In 2004, Tianhe District became the new city center of Guangzhou.

In 2010, the opening ceremony of Guangzhou Asian Games was held on a small island named Haixinsha in the Pearl River, and the Haixinsha Island is on the new axis of this city. It is said that the highest building, the largest public square, the largest underground space, the best cultural architecture and the most prosperous central business district locate here.

The Open Gene of Canton Fair

Guangzhou's stretching movement lies in not only the city's expansion, but also an open mind to the world. And it is the gene hidden inside the city's bone marrow and the city's unique spiritual temperament, which is mainly reflected in Canton Fair.

In 1957, the China Export Commodities Fair, an exhibition commonly called Canton Fair, was born in Guangzhou and opened a channel of communication between China and the world. The exhibition is "the No.1 exhibition in China" with the longest history, the highest level, the largest scale, the most complete types of goods, the largest number of buyers purchasing goods overseas and the best result of dealing.

Why should the first national exhibition of export commodities be held in Guangzhou? The reasons are unknown to outsiders. As a commercial city for thousands of years, Guangzhou has a strong commercial atmosphere, unique geographical advantages. It is the only channel for businessmen form Hong Kong, Macao and Southeast Asian to do business in the Chinese mainland.

In the early 1970s, Canton Fair was put into service in the new exhibition hall on Liuhua Road. Liuhua Pavilion is quite close to Guangzhou Railway Station, and keeps the Baiyun Airport within five or six kilometers' range of driving (but now it has moved from the city center to further suburbs, and it is called New Baiyun Airport to show the difference). In 1986, Liuhua Pavilion and its surrounding modern buildings such as Dongfang Hotel, Liuhua Hotel, the new Guangzhou Railway Station were named "Liuhua Yuyu", one of the eight attractions in Guangzhou.

Goat in the Chinese culture represents tameness. Because "goat" is pronounced the same with "sun" in Chinese, "goat" gets the meaning of auspiciousness. Because of a legend about goat, Guangzhou is also known as "Yangcheng". Since the beginning of Song Dynasty, people in the city has continually selected the eight attractions of the city, which called "Eight Attractions of Guangzhou".

In April 2001, in the eastern part of Pazhou which is more than 10 kilometers away from the Liuhua Pavilion, a new exhibition center was being constructed, and it was put into use in 2003. In October 2008, the 104th Canton Fair was held in Pazhou Complex.

Pazhou, the location of Huangpu Ancient Port, with Pazhou Convention and Exhibition Center, once again became a symbol of the communication between Guangzhou and the world.

With the arrival of the Internet era, Canton Fair also innovates constantly. It builds e-commerce platform to create an year-round online Canton Fair. Canton Fair embraces the Internet, so does Pazhou. Dozens of enterprises including Tencent, Alibaba, MIUI, Vipshop and so on gather in the agglomeration area of Internet innovations on the west side of Pazhou Island to set up headquarters or project companies.

WeChat is among them. The company WeChat belongs to is Tencent.

▲ Pazhou Convention and Exhibition Center once again become a symbol of the communication between Guangzhou and the world.

Before the emergence of WeChat, their social software QQ was once the most popular one. Tencent purchased a piece of land in Pazhou at the price of 17.6 billion to build the headquarters building of WeChat, which is perhaps a way to show business ambitions.

It is believed that even after many years, Chinese people will remember in this era there is a social networking software called WeChat, which has a profound impact on their daily life. With " To connect everything " as its slogan, WeChat has become a software most Chinese people will install in their smart phones in this era. For a long time, it makes a lot of Chinese people do not need cash in their wallets, because online payment is so popular that you can pay directly by means of scanning QR codes even in a small shop in China ' s remote rural areas. The entire transaction process is done without cash.

In the second quarter of 2016, WeChat has already been installed in more than 94% of smart phones in China, and monthly active users have reached to 0.806 billion. Besides, its users cover more than 200 countries and speak more than 20 languages.

WeChat was born in Guangzhou. It connects China with the world in a special way , making the world more open.

WeChat and QQ are only Tencent's most representative products. Ma Huateng, the person in charge of this company, in the early stage of his business leads his own team to design webpages, to do system integration, and to do programming. But because of knowing nothing about marketing operation, they are often shut out when they promote their products to operators. Such experience, whether Bill Gates or Steve Jobs, should have been experienced.

In October 2016, the total number of China Mobile Net users in China has reached 1.077 billion, and the number of mobile Internet users is up to 1.02 billion, reaching a new record in its history, which is second to none in the world.

People bring the experience of the using Internet from the earlier desktop PC to all aspects of work and life. All areas can be always realtime online. With the use of WeChat, all industries are provided with a good foundation to develop online and offline businesses, which means a lot of opportunities. And the changes WeChat and its similar products bring to China are still on the way, far from ending.

Free Trade Zone: "the Welding Spot" Jointing the World

Draw a circle with Nansha as the center and 50 km as the radius circle. Such circle can include all major cities in the Pearl River Delta, including all ports and wharfs in Hong Kong and Macau. With a radius of 100 km the circle covers 9 cities in the Pearl River Delta and 5 major international airports. Geographically, Nansha is the center of the Pearl River Delta. But it is far from the economic development center. In China where it is believed that "Development is the absolute principle", Nansha seems to have verified the Chinese saying "black light" which means something locating at the center is intentionally or unintentionally ignored. In the 1980s, the wasteland Nansha, known as the "Siberia" in Guangzhou, is bleak and lifeless.

Huo Yingdong, an industrialist in Hong Kong, did not think so. Starting with lightering, and then engaging in real estate, he initiated the pattern of installment commonly used in the whole country. When he died in 2006, the official announcement was that he is "a close friend of the Chinese Communist Party", and in the eyes of Chinese people he is a trusted patriot. Like many Hong Kong people, Huo Yingdong's ancestral home is in Guangdong. He once built the Luoxi Bridge for his hometown Panyu in Guangzhou, so that the Pearl River no longer blocks the communication between two sides.

Huo Yingdong devoted huge sums of money and a lot of effort to Nansha. During his lifetime he repeatedly said that he had a "Nansha dream", and hoped to construct Nansha into an open window of Guangdong and even the whole country.

In 1992, Huo Yingdong bought 22 square kilometers of land in the coastal area of Nansha for operation and development. Since 2002, Nansha Hotel, World Trade Center and other landmarks as well as Dongfa Port, Nansha Coach Terminal, Humen Ferry Terminal, Nansha Information Technology Park had been constructed one after another. It is said that Huo Yingdong has invested 6 billion yuan within 25 years in Nansha. Such an amount of money is worth two Canton Tower (a shapely TV tower more than 400 meters), the landmark building of Guangzhou, or a tourist town covering an area of nearly 100 million square meters inland.

Solely relying on an enterprise, the speed of developing a vast land cannot be forcibly said to be fast, even though it cannot be said to be slow.

90% of the developed cities in the world locate in coastal areas. For example, in the United States, the most powerful country in the world, New York, Boston, Philadelphia, Washington, Seattle, San Francisco, Los Angeles, Houston, Atlanta, Miami are all coastal areas. The whole country of Japan is situated in a narrow coastal area. In the past, the development of Guangzhou has been dependent on the coastal areas of the Pearl River. Guangzhou is built near water and developed on water. However, with the development of the city, Guangzhou must move from relying on water to relying on the sea. As the only region nearing the sea in Guangzhou, Nansha undoubtedly becomes the core of its development.

Everything goes well! Nansha, together with Huo family, waits for a new opportunity. Now it seems that perhaps this opportunity should be called "Free Trade Zone".

In December 2014, the State Council decided to set up China (Guangdong) Pilot Free Trade Zone, Guangdong Free Trade Zone covers three areas: Nansha New Area in Guangzhou (Guangzhou Nansha Free Trade Zone), Qianhai and Shekou Area in Shenzhen (Shenzhen Free Trade Zone of Qianhai and Shekou), Hengqin New Area in Zhuhai (Zhuhai Hengqin Free Trade Zone), with a total area of 1162 square kilometers.

China Free Trade Zone is a new node for China to deepen reform and opening-up. Set up outside the customs and within the boundary of China, with tax preference and policies for special customs supervision as the main means and the trade liberalization and convenience as the main purpose, it is a multi-functional special economic zone. On September 29, 2013 China (Shanghai) Pilot Free Trade Zone was officially established, becoming the first free trade zone in China.

China (Guangdong) Pilot Free Trade Zone locates in three cities including Guangzhou, Shenzhen and Zhuhai. Guangzhou Nansha New Area covers an area of 60 square kilometers (including the area of 7.06 square kilometers of Guangzhou Nansha Bonded Port Area).

There is a detailed introduction to Nansha Pilot Free Trade Zone on the official website of Guangzhou Nansha New Area in China

(Guangdong) Pilot Free Trade Zone: Nansha Pilot Free Trade Zone is committed to building a kind of legal international business environment in accordance with the new system of international rules, taking the lead in achieving service trade liberalization with Hong Kong and Macao, building an international shipping and logistics center with a high level of integration of international trade and financial innovation services, creating a demonstration base of the cooperation in technology and innovation between countries and regions along Maritime Silk Road, building a twoway channel and an important platform for Hong Kong and Macao to develop the mainland market and for the mainland via Hong Kong and Macao to develop international market, and playing an important role in building the new pattern of open economy.

Nansha Pilot Free Trade Zone is the first to implement the new model of "one counter handles all necessary formalities". It is the first in the country to expand the reform of "one business license one code" to 13 departments including industry and commerce, quality supervision, state tax and others, the first to provide the inspection service of government purchases, the first to implement the mechanism of customs quick inspection and release, and the first to create "wisdom inspection port".

Nansha Pilot Free Trade Zone created a remarkable "Speed of Free Trade Zone" in Guangdong.

Shenzhen:
A " Young " City
Keeps up with the
World

The Great Changes
of a Small Fishing Village

How long does it take for a small fishing village to develop into a large city? The answer Shenzhen gives is 30 years.

The Chinese take delight in sortation and ordering, such as the four major inventions and the five greatest warriors, and the city is the case. In the 1990s, people were used to abbreviating the three largest cities to "Jing-Jin-Hu" (Beijing, Tianjin and Shanghai). But in the beginning of this century, the three greatest cities referred to "Bei-Shang-Guang" (Beijing, Shanghai and Guangzhou). Around 2010, people were more accustomed to referring to the greatest cities as "Beijing, Shanghai, Guangzhou and Shenzhen" . The up-and-coming youngster—Shenzhen has become a super city in China's city pattern and been widely accepted.

The supporters of special economic zones can say some successful examples, among them the most successful one is the one near Hong Kong and later known as the "Shenzhen miracle".

Because of the consideration of possible risks, China did not Shenzhen: A "Young" City Keeps up with the World dare to implement economic reforms on a national scale. So, Shenzhen Special Economic Zone was established to do the test. Unexpectedly, it attracted thousands of foreign investors. The tested policy was immediately extended to other cities, including Shanghai subsequently.

Shenzhen has produced the first stock in China, auctioned the land market for the first time, created many new terms and lifestyles such as boss, going into business, stock company, migrant worker, fry cuttlefish and job-hopping. Over the past 30 years, Shenzhen has created innumerable "No. 1 in China".

The beginning of the reform in Shenzhen originates from the cry for the construction of Shekou adjoining the bay. Yuan Geng is the most dazzling name in the history of Shenzhen Special Economic Zone and even the history of China's reform and opening-up. His keen determination on reform of and all kinds of exploration for Shekou industrial area seem to

▲ Luohu Port is located at the southern part of Luohu business center in Shenzhen. Separated from Hong Kong by a narrow river, Shenzhen is joined to Hong Kong through a two-decker foot bridge and a railway bridge. Luohu Port is one of the only two land ports in Shenzhen before reform and opening-up. Photographer: Da Guang

▲ The Photo of Shenzhen shot from a high angle. Photographer: Wang Yubo

still have a significance on the present day.

China Merchants Bureau links the high-ranking offical in late Qing Dynasty Li Hongzhang in 1872 with the communist Yuan Geng in 1978.

In 1872, Li Hongzhang wrote a memorial to Tongzhi to request the establishment of the China Merchants, and the memorial was approved three days later. In October 1978, Yuan Geng, as the 29th head of the China Merchants Group, submitted *the Consultation on the Full Use of Hong Kong Merchants* to the Central Committee of the Communist Party of China, requesting the establishment of Shekou Industrial Zone, and the request was also approved three days later.

In 1978, Yuan Geng was 61 years old, the age called "a cycle of sixty years" in China. At this age, many people may have enjoyed their old age in peace, but Yuan Geng's new business has just begun.

He set up a board with words "Time is money, efficiency is life" on the road in Shekou, trying to break the life-long cadre employment system. And he published those articles which directly criticized him by pointing out his name in the newspaper. Faced with unwarranted accusations, Yuan Geng difficultly but also firmly carried out the reform in Shekou, from economic to political field, from social to cultural field.

Shekou's development and change is the epitome of Shenzhen's reform and opening-up.

From 1979 to 1988, during the ten years when he was in charge of the work in Shenzhen Special Economic Zone, the former Vice Premier of the State Council, Gu Mu, successively visited the Shenzhen Special Economic Zone for 12 times. Almost all major decisions in the early stage the special economic zone

▲ Shenzhen Stock Exchange was opened on December 1st in 1990. Rooted in the frontier of China's reform and opening-up, serving China's economic development strategies, Shenzhen Stock Exchange is committed to build the most dynamic capital market platform in the world. Photographer: Da Guang

were formulated and implemented with his participation.

Wu Nansheng, who was responsible for the preparation of three special economic zones in Guangdong Province, first put forward "Guangdong takes the first step". And with the firm determination—"Kill me if you need to kill someone.", he took the initiative to apply for special economic zone.

Of course, the person most remembered with gratitude by people in Shenzhen is Deng Xiaoping. He named Shenzhen "Special Economic Zone", which occurred during the time from January 24 to February 5 in 1984, the time when Deng Xiaoping came to Guangdong to inspect Shenzhen.

Deng Xiaoping is the chief architect of China's economic and social reforms. In China, people are more willing to respectfully and courteously call him "Comrade Xiaoping".

In November 2000, a statue of Deng Xiaoping, was unveiled on the top of Lianhua Mountain in Shenzhen. It is the first statue of Deng Xiaoping approved by central government and erected in the form of urban sculpture in China.

The bronze statue of Deng Xiaoping on the top of Lianhua Mountain is 6 meters high and weighs 6 tons. The shaped Xiaoping is wearing a windbreaker, facing the south and striding forward, with a corner of the windbreaker flowing behind. When you climb from the north of Lianhua Mountain to the top of the mountain, the first thing come to your sight is the screen wall engraved with Deng Xiaoping's original words: "Shenzhen' s

▲ Located in Shenzhen, the giant portrait of Deng Xiaoping, has become one of the signs of Shenzhen. Many domestic and foreign tourists come here to cherish the memory of the old man who has changed China.

development and experience have proved that our policy of establishing special economic zones is correct." The other side of the screen wall is write with clerical script, "I am a son of the Chinese people, and I deeply love my country and people in my country."

Around 1990, the international and domestic situation underwent profound changes. The development of the special economic zones, the reform and opening-up was again faced with obstacles. At such a critical moment, Deng Xiaoping once again came to Guangdong for inspection. It was during January 19 to January 29 in 1992 when he spent four days in

Shenzhen and seven days in Zhuhai. On January 18 to February 21, Deng Xiaoping delivered important speeches in Wuchang, Shenzhen, Zhuhai, Shanghai and other places. He put forward the requirement of "taking advantage of good opportunities to speed up the pace of reform and opening-up, striving for a new level of national economy", which laid the ideological foundation for China to embark on the road of development of socialist market economy with Chinese characteristics.

On January 21, in China World Trade Center, Deng Xiaoping delivered the most important speech in the process of inspection. "China needs to be vigilant against the Right deviation, but primarily, it should guard against the 'Left' deviation. It has taken the special economic zones more than ten years to reach the present stage. They can collapse overnight! People will believe and support you only when the economy get developed and their lives become better. We must firmly adhere to the party's basic line of taking economic development as the central task not for ten years, twenty years but for a hundred years! The ways of not adhering to socialism, not reforming and opening-up, not developing the economy and not improving people's lives are all dead ends!"

The International Trade Building is known as the "the window of Shenzhen Special Economic Zone" and "a symbol of China's reform and opening up".

In 1984, the International Trade Building with a height of 160 meters and a total of 53 layers was completed after the construction was conducted for 14 months, creating a "three-days-a-floor" miracle. After the main building was started constructing, at the beginning it took 7 days to build a layer , then 5 days and then 4 days. From the 30th floor , the speed kept at three days one floor. The widespread "Shenzhen speed" as a result of the International Trade Building has become a new concept of high speed and high efficiency, and a symbol of China's construction and development after reforming and opening up.

The City of Immigrants

In just 30 years, Shenzhen has transformed from a small border town with a population of 3 million people and two or three narrow streets into a modern city with a population of 10 million people, prosperous economy, harmonious society, complete functions and beautiful environment, creating a miracle in the history of industrialization, urbanization and modernization of the world.

In Shenzhen's development process, there are more unknown people who make special contributions to the construction of this city. These contributions are seemingly insignificant but real, and become a great force to promote the city forward, which is in accordance with the Chinese ancient poem "Silent and soft, it moistens everything". This poem means that the spring rain quietly falls at night in the spring breeze, quietly moistening all things on the earth.

Shenzhen is the most typical immigrant city in China. In 1979, when Shenzhen was at the early stage of construction, the population was only thirty-odd million. By the end of 2015, the resident population has reached 113,789 million. Shenzhen has become a veritable city of immigrants and the largest immigrant city in China.

In July 1982, 20,000 infrastructure-construction engineering corps from Shanghai, Tianjin, Tangshan and other places assembled and went down south. They all transferred to construction workers, and a quarter of high buildings in Shenzhen in the 20th century was constructed by them.

In a sense, Shenzhen's history of 30 years is Shenzhen immigrants' history of struggling. They come here with dreams from all parts of the country. They grow out of nothing. They go through struggles, prosperity, confusion and transformation, enjoy the happiness of success and meet the new challenges together with the city.

The praise for these people in 2009 reached a special climax. In 2009, *Time* magazine in the United States selected Person of the Year, and Chinese workforce is one of them.

▲ The night scene of Shenzhen. Photographer: Wang Yubo

As the only group on the list, Chinese workforce ranks second only to the Federal Reserve Chairman. *Time* magazine has such a comment: "There is one word 'keeping 8%' in China. This word means maintaining an annual economic growth rate of 8%, which is essential to ensure social stability form the point view of the Chinese government. Many years ago, many people think this is a dream, but China has made it. As one of the major economic entities in the world, China continues maintaining the fastest pace of development, and leads the world to economic resurgence. These credits should first go to thousands of hard-working and persevering Chinese workers.

Whether in history or at present, Chinese workers are a great, outstanding and contributory team. Since the founding of new China, especially in the 30 years after reforming and opening-up, thousands of Chinese works have worked hard and made great contributions, paying an important role in promoting the economic development and social progress of China.

The City of Innovation

In 2015, Huawei applied for 52, 550 domestic patents and 30,613 foreign patents, with the total number of patent applications ranking first in the world. In 2015, Huawei, with the number of 3898, topped the list of patent rankings of global enterprises.

However, the number of applications does not mean the accumulation and advantages of a company on the aspect of patents. Only authorized patents can have real power! This is the reason why in 2015, Apple licensed 98 patents to Huawei in 2015, while Huawei licensed 769 patterns to Apple.

With the excellent quality, the newly born Huawei phones catch up with Apple and Samsung in the Chinese market.

Founded in 1987, Huawei Technologies Co. Ltd. is a private communications technology company which produces and sells communications equipment. At the end of 2016, he has more than 170,000 employees. Huawei's products and solutions have been applied in more than 170 countries around the world, serving for 45 operators out of the top 50 and 1/3 of the population of the world. In terms of the countries and population Huawei serves for, it is a global company with headquarters based in Shenzhen. It is a company developed from Shenzhen.

Huawei has become a symbol of innovation in Shenzhen and an exhibition displaying city's innovation and development. Shenzhen has

▲ Founded in 2006, DJI-Innovations (abbreviated as DJI), is the leading developer and producer of the control system and solutions of unmanned aerial vehicles. Photographer: Wang Yubo

been born for innovation, becoming the "City of Makers" and "City of Innovation" in the eyes of Chinese people. In addition to Huawei, there are some other famous companies in Shenzhen such as ZTE, Tencent, DJI and BGI.

Founded in 1998, Tencent, is one of the largest Internet integrated service providers, but also one of the Internet companies with most service users in China. China's service users. The most well-known products of Tencent are QQ and WeChat. To some extent, these two products have already had their own implications, just like Chinese people will not only consider Apple to be a kind of fruits but also an American company and the products it produced.

The chairman of the board of Tencent, Ma Huateng, came to Shenzhen at the age of 13. In 1998, with 500,000 yuan of funds, he and his team of five people developed QQ software. Capital and technology have ever become the bottleneck of the development of Tencent, which made Ma Huateng sleepless all night. At the most difficult time, he wanted to sell QQ several times, but he insisted on keeping it. And the result turned out that in June 2015, the market value of Tencent ranked fifth in global Internet companies and the annual income of 2014 was 78.9 billion yuan.

The innovative and entrepreneurial DJI in field of advanced technology and BGI are considered examples of innovation in Shenzhen. DJI is known as the top-level company in the field of UAV with a global market share of more than 50%. Its products have been used for aerial photography, film, agriculture, news, energy, remote sensing mapping and many other areas, and continuing to integrate into new industries. BGI benefits human beings through the genetic science and technology. Founded in 1999, this company is the largest genomics research and development institution. It leads the development of genomics by means of the new developing pattern of " production-teaching-research" integration. Through the extensive cooperation between the branches around the world and the industry chain, BGI applies the frontier achievements in scientific research to medical health, agricultural breeding, resource preservation and other fields to promote the transformation of gene technology achievements, and further to benefit all people. BGI is selected into Global

Growth Companies in 2015. General speaking, Global Growth Companies are regarded as market pioneers, innovators and builders.

It is not comprehensive to consider that the innovative ability of Shenzhen is represented by these well-known companies. "Independent innovation" has become the leading strategy for the development of the city. The research spending of Shenzhen is increasing year by year, with a proportion of 4.05% of GDP in 2015, which is twice the national average. PCT (Patent Cooperation Treaty) international patent applications and the invention patent ownership per ten thousand people of Shenzhen are at the first place among large and medium-sized cities in China. Besides, the innovation ability of Shenzhen finds a front position in the world in the

▲ In 2015, the first "National Public Entrepreneurship and Innovation Week" of China was held. In 2016, the "National Public Entrepreneurship and Innovation Week" became big event of innovation industry. The picture shows the intelligent robot displayed on the "National Public Entrepreneurship and Innovation Week". Photographer: Wang Yubo fields of 4G technology, gene sequencing, metamaterials and 3D display.

In 2014, Shenzhen PCT international patent applications reached 11600 with an increase of 15.9%, ranking first in large and medium-sized cities in China for 11 consecutive years. The invention patent ownership per ten thousand people reached 66.7, ranking first among major cities of China. In the list of ten Chinese innovators released by Forbes, Shenzhen accounted for 5 people. In 2014, two research results of Shenzhen were selected into the top ten scientific progress in China. Enterprises have become the major market players of Shenzhen and innovative actors.

As the most unique innovative city on the chain of global innovation, the youngest city in the first-tier cities in China, Shenzhen has been constantly exploring new economic growth impetus and developing the most suitable stage for global makers.

The Copycat Goes Away, the Wisdom Returns

After 30 years of reform and opening up, Shenzhen has had a relatively perfect downstream industry chain and formed a gathering area of science and technology, capital, information and talents in the field of hardware. When talking about his original intention of starting a business in Shenzhen, the founder of Seeed Studio, which is the largest open source hardware manufacturer in China, Pan Hao said that he was impressed by the prefect hardware in Shenzhen when he went around a whole day in Huaqiang North Commercial Area. Cyril Ebersweiler, the founder of the hardware incubation center HAXLR8R, an internationally renowned organization, moved its headquarters from Silicon Valley to Shenzhen. He said, "I can find any needed raw materials within 1 kilometer, which is impossible in the United States, Europe and even any other places in the world, because Huaqiang North Commercial Area can not be found in any other places." Another Indian businessman who settled in Shenzhen also

▲ Shatoujiao is prosperous in business for its unique geographic location. Photographer: Da Gunag

said that any design, no matter how complex it is, can be produced in less than a week.

In Shenzhen, you can find any needed raw materials in the area less than 1 km away from Huaqiang North Commercial Area, and you can complete the whole process of "prototype-product-small batch production" within one week with only 1% to 5% of the cost in Silicon Valley. An entrepreneur who started a business in Zhongguancun asked his son: "Why must we go all the way to Shenzhen to start a business?" The son replied that it took only two weeks to find an IC in Shenzhen, but in other places the time spent may be two months. And there are many processing factories in Shenzhen and its surrounding areas. They produce good-quality and cheap PCB boards. This is an advantage of industrial chain that Shenzhen realized through the combination of the basic manufacturing industry and developed market economy. Such advantage makes the innovation in Shenzhen more convenient, making Shenzhen a "Paradise of Makers".

Huaqiang North Commercial Area ever received about 500,000 people per day on average and the its annual turnover was more than 300 billion yuan. It was the largest high-tech electronic products trading center with the most complete product categories and the largest annual turnover. And it was once regarded as the "weather vane" and "barometer" of China's electronics industry. Here the turnover of electronic components accounted for 95% of the total number of electronic communications market in Shenzhen.

However, under huge turnovers, a variety of bogus electronic products are also emerging. After an Apple mobile phone comes into market, a month later you may spend several hundred yuan to buy a very similar phone with a new trademark of a bitten orange in Huaqiang North Commercial Area. With low price and fast updated speed, they shatter those domestic mobile phone brands which need both internal testing and network testing to pieces.

Therefore, Huaqiang North was once regarded as a pronoun of "shanzhai" and got into trouble by the name of the largest place producing fake mobile phones.

Copycat is usually called "shanzhai" in China. "Shanzhai" originally means the walled city in the mountain, and more often it refers to the product accused of imitation, copy and plagiarism.

If we say that copycat mobile phones can also make a profit, in the era of copycat tablet computers, a tablet computer at the price of about 200 yuan is everywhere. By selling copycat phones and tablet computers at low prices, copycat manufacturers quickly take roots and grow in Shenzhen, and then they are forced by low prices to shut down their companies and withdraw from the market.

Copycat and innovation are the two sides of a coin. Wang Jian, the chairman of the technical committee of Alibaba says in the book *Being Online*, "When most people ignore middle and small-sized enterprises like Huaqiang North, more people think these enterprises are fake, and we believe that they are promoting industrial changes."

▲ China Hi-Tech Fair, the largest and most influential science and technology exhibition in present China, is held every year in Shenzhen and said to be the "First Science and Technology Exhibition in China". The fair has become an important window for the opening-up of China's hi-tech field. It plays an increasingly important role in promoting the commercialization, industrialization and internationalization of the achievements of high and new technology as well as promoting economic and technological exchanges and cooperation between countries and regions. Photographer: Wang Yubo

Neil Goshenfield, the founder of Fab Lab believes that copycat is also a good way of innovation. He says that he likes Huaqiang North, and he has bought his son a product like AppleWatch which is better than AppleWatch and equipped with functions of mobile phones. It is also a kind of advanced technology to produce such a watch with many functions. In Fab2.0, we can also do some individuation manufacturing. Design, model and pack all functions to study how to copy this function instead of making a fake AppleWatch. "Here copy means that you have ability to go beyond the functional scope of the product."

At the end of 2010, Shenzhen began to organize crackdowns against intellectual property infringement and the production and sale of counterfeit and shoddy goods. After more than six months of crackdowns, more than 3600 merchants in Huaqiang North electronics market withdrew from the market, leading to a large-scale reshuffle of the mobile phone industry.

In addition, due to the construction of Shenzhen Metro Line 7, since March 2013, the main road in Huaqiang North was blocked for reconstruction. In Huaqiang North there once appeared the scene of vacant shops and declining rents.

▲ Huaqiang North Commercial Street.

At the end of 2016, Huaqiang North was opened again, making a stage pose as "pedestrian street" for the first time. Over the past 30 years, Huaqiang North has grown into "The First Street of China Electronics". In the next five to ten years, Huaqiang North will be committed to become "the most influential high-end electronic information service, display and trading center which radiates both home and abroad in China, a diversified and mixed high-quality commercial center , a manufacturing service center, and an integrated area with both business offices and living conditions".

Shenzhen has a clear understanding of innovation. Shenzhen intends to establish a comprehensive innovation ecosystem, and combine all kinds of innovative elements to form a positive oscillation through the innovation chain, that is, investing research funds earliest, and finally coming down through the results and financial innovations, and then returning to scientific research and innovation for a new round of innovation of higher technology and higher level. And a positive oscillation is thus formed.

Foshan:
A Blessed City

Chinese Cuisine
Goes out
of China

Shunde, together with Dongguan, Zhongshan and Nanhai, is called "Four Tigers in Guangdong" and at the first place of the top one hundred areas in China in 2014. In China's basic discourse system, the leading position in a list indicates the city's uniqueness.

Shunde, which means "following the way of Heaven and practicing morality", is a district of Foshan City, Guangdong Province. Since ancient times it has experienced developed economy, business prosperity as well as cultural and educational heyday.

▲ Chencun rice noddle is a traditional dish of Chencun Town, Shunde District, Foshan City, Guangdong Province. Photographer: Lu Kaiyang

▶ The roast suckling pig is glazed and cooked slowly over an open fire, and its skin is crisp and the fat is not greasy. With outstanding taste, Shunde Jun'an steamed pig and roast pig become the most well-known roast suckling pig. Photographer: Lu kaiyang

In December 2014, UNESCO awarded Shunde a plaque with words "Capital of Food"on it, so Shunde officially became a member of UNESCO Creative Cities Network.

At that time, there are six cities awarded the name of "Capital of Food" by the UNESCO in the world, namely, Popayan in Colombia, Chengdu in China, Ostersund in Sweden, Zahlah in Lebanon, Jeonju in South Korea and Shunde in Foshan, China.

Singh, director of the UNESCO office in Beijing, said, "Shunde, as a representative of Cantonese cuisine, has a very superior character and Shunde restaurants are around the world, which is very important for Shunde food to go abroad. In the future, we will also provide a more international platform to take Shunde food to the whole world."

Food has become one of the most important labels of Shunde, the city with an area of less than 1000 square kilometers. Chinese people show special preference for food culture, so there is an ancient proverb "Food is the first necessity of man.".

Cantonese cuisine is one of the Four Major Chinese Cuisines.

Cantonese cuisine in the narrow sense refers to the Guangzhou cuisine, including Shun (de), Nan(hai) and Pan (yu).

Cantonese cuisine is famous in the world because of its strict selection of materials, fine workmanship, combination of Chinese and Western styles, delicious taste, health and other characteristics. As the most influential Chinese cuisine overseas, Cantonese restaurants are around the world, so there is a saying "Where there are ethnic Chinese there are Cantonese cuisine.".

Shunde, one of the five districts of Foshan, is one of the most important birthplace of Cantonese cuisine. Shunde's food culture is also a microcosm of Foshan. Roughly registered chefs and bakers are nearly a thousand in Foshan City, and many of them are national super-class master chef.

The statistics in 2014 show that Shunde, one of the places where there are most domestic chefs and noted restraurants, has 9 Chinese master chefs, 34 Chinese cooking teachers, 21 famous Chinese restaurants and 11 kinds of famous Chinese snacks. In 2004 it was chosen as "Hometown of Chinese Chefs" by the Chinese Cuisine Association. In 2010 it was named as "City of Chinese Food". In Shunde, one of every 17 people may work in the restaurant industry.

For a century, many well-known chefs appear in the Foshan restaurant industry. Tao Taoju, Qimiaozhai and Datong restaurants, which were set up by Tan Jienan in the 1920s to 1930s, are still renowned in Guangzhou.

"Taotaoju" means delightedly drinking tea in the restaurant. Taotaoju, mainly engaged in tea-drinking and dining, is one of the most famous restaurants in Guangzhou. Cantonese people like drinking tea, especially drinking morning tea in restaurants. After guests sit down, the waiter come up and ask guests to order tea or pastries. Morning tea has become a unique urban culture in Guangzhou.

The famous chefs in the 1930s to 1950s, Cui Qiang, Li He, Wang Rui and Lu Zhen were known as the Four Heavenly Kings in Guangdong catering industry, and in the 1950s to 1960s there were Luo Kun and Pan Tong.

It is rare that the team of the two national chefs in Shunde, Xiao Liangchu and Kang Hui, successively set up state banquets in Beijing and Shanghai. From 1951 Xiao Liangchu as the chief chef worked in the national guesthouse in China, Shanghai Jinjiang Hotel, cooking and arranging dishes for the king, president, prime minister and prime minister from more than 100 countries.

In 1954 Premier Zhou Enlai attended the Geneva Conference, accompanied by Xiao Liangchu as a chef. Premier Zhou invited comedian Chaplin to dinner, and they talked delightedly. Chaplin finished eating and longed for more, so he specifically invited Xiao Liangchu to cook crisp fried chicken for packaging and sharing with families.

In 1961, Premier Chou Enlai led the Chinese delegation to attend the Geneva Enlarged Conference. Xiao Liangchu was asked to be the chef. His specialty Salt Baked Eight-Flavour Chicken was complimented by the guests from every contry.

Kang Hui was once the executive chef of the Beijing Hotel. He was responsible for the construction of the Diaoyutai State Guesthouse and the restaurant of the Great Hall of the People. In 2002, he was awarded one of the 12 Chinese master chefs in China.

Chinese Kung Fu Goes Abroad

In 1999 *Time* magazine made a list of heroes and idols in the 20th century. On the list, there are the late British Princess Diana, the boxing champion Ali, Marilyn Monroe, US President Kennedy and Pele. But for Chinese, the most familiar one should be the yellow-skinned kung fu star Bruce Lee who often looks recalcitrant when he takes pictures. Like Michael Jordan is a sign

▲ Kung fu star Bruce Lee.

of basketball and Bailey is a sign of modern football, Bruce Lee is the best endorser of Chinese Kung Fu.

In 2000, the US government announced the release of a *Bruce Lee's 60th anniversary commemorative stamps*. Bruce Lee became the third artist after Marilyn Monroe and 007, and also the first Chinese who won this award. In 2003 the American magazine *Black Belt* launched the 30th anniversary of the death of Bruce Lee, indicating "Bruce Lee's long-term influence on American martial arts".

In English, Chinese martial arts are called kung fu, which is originally proverb of martial arts in the central region of Foshan and the Pearl River Delta. In language translation, the word-for-word transliteration may because it is difficult to translate or it is more important. Kung Fu clearly belongs to the latter. Undoubtedly it is Bruce Lee who make the world fall in love with Chinese Kung Fu.

Bruce Lee' s ancestral home is in the town of Jun'an in Shunde, Guangdong, the hometown of kung fu. The largest Bruce Lee Memorial Hall in the world is in Jun'an. In 2008 the large exhibition hall with a total area of 370,000 square meters was shown to the public.

Foshan is the main source of southern Chinese martial arts. In 2004, Foshan was awarded the title of "City of Martial Arts". In the early Ming Dynasty, Foshan Kung Fu was quite popular. At the end of the Qing Dynasty and the beginning of the Republic of China, there were various schools of martial arts and appeared a group of martial arts masters and organizations with international influence. They went abroad and became globalized though various channels. Many kinds of Chinese boxing and schools such as the widespread Choy Lee Fut, Hong Boxing, Wing Chun are rooted in Foshan. The ancestral home of famous martial arts master Huang Feihong, Liang Zan, the master of Wing Chun, and Yip Man are also in Foshan.

Bruce Lee is well known to many people. He is a pioneer of the change of martial arts, martial arts attacker, martial arts philosopher, the founder of UFC, the father of MMA father, martial arts master, founder of martial arts films, founder of Jeet Kune Do, Chinese film actor of martial arts, the first global promoter of Chinese martial arts and the first Chinese Hollywood actor. His four and a half films in Hong Kong broke many records for three times. Among them, the film *Way of the Dragon* broke the record of Asian film box office. The global total box office of the film

▲ The Wing Chun master Yip Man who learned and became a master in Foshan is renowned at home and abroad.

Way of the Dragon shot through the cooperation with Hollywood reached 2.3 billion US dollars. The American newspaper even described Bruce Lee as "Kung Fu King", and the Japanese called him "Warrior Saint", while Hong Kong newspapers praised him as "Wizard of modern Chinese Kung Fu and in the film history".

It is after Bruce Lee when many Chinese stars of martial arts step on the world stage. Jackie Chan and Jet Li are among them.

Different from Bruce Lee, who directly shows the firmness of Kung Fu, Jackie Chan connects martial arts with opera juggling, which reduces bloody violence scenes commonly seen in martial arts films while paying attention to the viewing quality of actions, and opens a new space of Kung Fu comedies.

Looking back to the past, Bruce Lee was born in the United States, but his childhood and youth was spent in Hong Kong. The little Bruce Lee was very thin and weak. In order to build up his body, his father taught him to play tai chi. Bruce Lee himself was fond of trying new things and adventure, especially outdoor sports. So, he completely fell in love with martial arts. In addition to tai chi, he also learned Wing Chun, Hong Boxing and Shaolin Boxing, laying foundation for the future creation.

In 1967, at the age of 27, Bruce Lee founded the world-wide modern Chinese Kung Fu Jeet Kune Do which is without the limitation of schools in the United States. This is a kind of all-round free sparring combining the essence of various martial arts in the world. But many people think that Jeet Kune Do resembles Wing Chun to some extent. There is no doubt that such resemblance comes from his teacher Yip Man.

The ancestral home of Yip Man, born in 1893, is in Sang Yuan in Nanhai County, Guangdong. In the 1950s, he began to teach Wing Chun in Hong Kong. His disciples, Liang Ting, carried forward Wing Chun to

▲ Yewen Hall collects and exhibits materials about how Yip Man carries forward Wing Chun.

the world, forming a set of the most authoritative traditional Chinese martial arts practice course *Wing Tsun* that is famous in the world. After Yip Man passed away in 1972, his two sons Ip Chun and Ip Ching were committed to promoting Wing Chun internationally. Ip Chun also won awards issued by US Olympic Committee.

Another Chinese Kung Fu star Jet Li was born in Beijing. He set a record for consecutively winning the all-round champion of Chinese martial arts in 1975 to 1979. Had not he starred in the film *Shaolin Temple* in 1982, he might be just a good martial arts player rather than a martial arts star.

The sensation caused by *Shaolin Temple* can be seen from the fact that the mainland the total domestic box office was up 100 million yuan with the ticket purchased at the price of 0.1 yuan. In other words, his film was watched at least 1 billion times.

The most classic movies shot starred by Jet Li are the series of *Once Upon a Time in China*. At the beginning of 90, Jet Li accepted the invitation of starring in *Once Upon a Time in China*, causing a sensation in Hong Kong, after which he starred in series of five *Once Upon a Time in China* films. In China, the movies shot on the theme of Fei-hung Wong are up to hundreds, creating a record in the world.

Of course, the character Fei-hung Wong in these films is not the same with the reality. Fei-hung Wong was born in Nanhai County, Foshan City in 1856. He is a master of Hong Boxing at the end of the Qing Dynasty and the beginning of the Republic of China and a grandmaster in the field of martial arts in Lingnan. He has an important influence on the development of southern Chinese martial arts. Fei-hung Wong is a legendary figure. He ever followed the famous patriotic generals Liu Yongfu in the anti-Japanese war to defend Taiwan. Also, he is a noted life-saving doctor with a big heart. What's more, he is good at lion dance and called Guangzhou lion king.

Dreams of Foshan

Food and martial arts make Foshan well-known in the world and become a cultural city and the core area of Cantonese culture. Equally important, Foshan is known as the national advanced manufacturing base and an important manufacturing center in Guangdong.

Foshan was started in Jin Dynasty and got the name in Tang Dynasty. 500 years ago, in the late Ming Dynasty in the traditional agricultural country, the division of labor in manufacturing process was more refined, and the class of handicraftsmen who broke away from agricultural

▲ Overlooking Foshan. Photographer: Li Xihua

cultivation appeared. At that time, the commodity economy was seeded in China, especially in the four places known as the "Four Famous Towns in Ancient China", namely, Hankow Town in Hubei, Jingdezhen in Jiangxi, Zhuxian Town in Henan and the known-to-us Foshan Town in Guangdong.

The city we are going to talk about is Foshan, a town that stepped onto the stage of Chinese history 500 years ago. It is during this period that Foshan rapidly developed into an economic, business and cultural center in Southern China.

During the Ming and Qing Dynasties, Foshan gradually developed into a goods distribution centers in Lingnan—to the area south of the Five Ridges, the manufacturing center of metallurgical casting, ceramics, textile, Chinese patent medicines.

Shiwan is located at the southeast of Chancheng District in Foshan, where, with the saying that "Shiwan tiles well-known overseas are the best in the world". The ceramic here has long been a bright "business card" of Foshan. In the Ming and Qing Dynasties, there are 107 ceramics with more than 60,000 people working in the nearby area for several kilometers around Shiwan Town. Because of Shiwan ceramics, Foshan is named "Pottery Capital in the South". "Du" in Chinese has a meaning of "leader" which means the best. After the reform and opening up, Shiwan ceramics are much more widely distributed, more diverse in kinds and larger in scales.

Even more incredibly, as a center of four kinds of manufacturing

▲ Shiwan ceramics enjoy high reputation. The picture shows visitors watching the exhibition in Foshan. Photographer: Li Xihua

industries, Foshan does not produce drug, cotton, iron mine and clay. Such phenomenon is vividly described as "creating something out of nothing".

As a matter of fact, the flourishment of the handicraft industry in Foshan has something to do with the southward migration of outcomers. In the late period of Southern Song Dynasty, in order to avoid wars, Chung Yuan population along with handicraftsmen moved to the South. In the Ming and Qing Dynasties, the development of handicraft industry in Foshan came to its peak. Handicraft industry spread all over more than 620 streets and 60 ferries, forming twenty-eight special commercial shops of all walks of life.

In 1872, the 36-year-old Chen Qiyuan from Jian Village in Xiqiao

Twon, Nanhai, Guangdong came back home from Southeast Asia. In the next year, by using self-designed machines, he founded the first national capital enterprise of silk reeling industry. At the age of 25, he went to Vietnam with his brother to do business. Perhaps in order to express the good expectation of "maintaining flourishment", he gave the factory the name of "Jichanglong".

Jichanglong Silk-Filature Factory was large in scale. Owing to good management, the business of the factory flourished, and its products were sold at home and abroad, bringing in a large amount of income. For the benefit of his hometown, he built luxurious "Baiye Lane" living buildings in Jian Village, which made him become a world-famous rich businessman.

Jichanglong Silk-Filature Factory is the first mechanized silk-filature factory run by national capital in China. Its establishment marked the beginning of a new historical period of the reeling industry, and promoted the development of the reeling industry in the Pearl River Delta and even the whole country.

Foshan also gave birth to first matches factory, Qiaomin Matches Factory, in China. In 1879 the young Wei Shengxuan, the founder of the factory, witnessed that the input of matches from abroad brought about the outflow of domestic wealth. Hence, he went to Japan to learn matches manufacturing techniques. After coming back home, he founded Qiaomin Matches Factory in Wenchangsha District in Foshan.

Symbolized by the first new-style silk-filature factory and matches factory in China, Foshan which leads new trends has become one of the birthplaces of modern national industry.

Today, Foshan has become one of the most important business centers in the Pearl River Delta Economic Zone, a national model city of logistics with a batch of logistics trading, a distribution center with large-scale investment and strong radiation capability. Foshan is one of the six China capital of brands, the exemplary city of the implementation of national trademark strategies and a city of brand economy in China. As a major manufacturing city, Foshan has a long history of industrial development, especially the traditional manufacturing industry, including Midea, Haitian and many other well-known enterprises with touring elements. Represented by Shiwan ceramics, the ceramic manufacturing industry owns hundreds of various types of industrial tiles and sanitary products. Represented by the watered gauze, illuminations and jade, the old-line art industry has become a perfect representative of humanity history. Represented by the Haitian soybean sauce and Shunde sugar, the food industry has witnessed the development process of food industry in Lingnan.

Dongguan: The Manufacturing City Facing Difficulties

The Miracle between Two Cities

Dongguan is located on the east coast of the Pearl River estuary. The Pearl River, the third largest river in China, flows into the sea via Guangdong, nourishing a few of cities, including Dongguan. These cities are known as the Pearl River Delta, which is one of most economically developed areas in China. In particular, Dongguan locates between the two major cities of Guangzhou and Shenzhen, within one-hour drive from the central urban area of Guangzhou and Shenzhen, but miraculously created a completely different way of growth form the two cities, keeping its own spirit.

One foreign expert once said, "More than 10 years ago, from the point of view of the satellite map, the area between Guangzhou and Shenzhen was blank. Within a few years, a city appeared in this blank." This is undoubtedly a miracle in the urban-construction and economic history of China.

Dongguan, whose fast development astonishes people, is the epitome of the development of Chinese cities and even China. Guancheng is a town in Dongguan. A town in China is a unit of administrative division at the level or below the level of county. Usually below a prefecture-level city is a county below which is a town. However, Dongguan has become a "special one". It is one of the few prefecture-level cities below which there are no districts and counties, commonly known as "Zhitongzi City".

▲ Dongguan is the historical and cultural city in Guangdong.

Guancheng is only one of more than 30 streets and towns in Dongguan, but it has always been the political, economic and cultural center of Dongguan City, with a long history and profound cultural heritage.

In China, cultural heritage is mainly reflected in the history of a city. Keyuan Garden, one of the four famous gardens in Qing Dynasty in Guangdong, a major historical and cultural site protected at the national level, is seated in the thousand-year-old ancient city. "Keyuan" means "can be visited and appreciated". Keyuan Garden was a gathering place for literati at that time. As a major historical and cultural site protected at the national level, Keyuan Garden takes an important place in the modern art and architectural history of Guangdong.

Chinese people are used to talking about Tang Poetry and Song Ci. Su Shi has received high attainments in the aspects of articles, poems and ci (a type of classical Chinese poetry in Song Dynasty). He can be called as the representative of the highest literary achievements of Song Dynasty. There is an unbeknown story between him and the Zifu Temple in Dongguan. He not only slept over in Zifu Temple, but also wrote three articles in 1100: *Memory in Arhat Pavilion in Zifu Temple in Dongguan County of Guangzhou, Inscription on the Stupa in Zifu Temple in Dongguan County of Guangzhou,* and *Praise for the Rebirth of the Cypress in Zifu Temple in*

▲ Guangdong Guanyinshan National Forest Park in Zhangmutou Town, Dongguan City

Dongguan County on Guangzhou, which are passed down to now.

Searching "Guancheng" in Baidu, you will first see the webpage titled "Cultural Guancheng", from which the unique status of culture in the city and traces left by the city can be seen. In fact, this is the official website of Wancheng Street Office. Baidu, most well-known in the field of network-searching, can be simply understood as google of China. Its name is said to be derived from a well-known Chinese poem, "Time and time again, I searched for you in the crowd. Suddenly, I spun around and saw the very you standing amidst thin lights." This poem is the representative works of a famous Ci writer in Song Dynasty. Isn't "searching for her time and time again" a true portrayal of network search.

The webpage introduces Guancheng like this: Guancheng Streets in Dongguan City have a long history of 1700 years. Since A.D. 757, it has been the location of the government of Dongguan city. It has a long history of culture and a lot of cultural relics.

Not Just "Destroying Opium at Humen Beach"

Dongguan is known to Chinese people partly because of "Destroying Opium at Humen Beach". In the 1880s, due to the sharp increase in opium input, the trade status of China and Britain changed completely, with Britain changing from import surplus into the export surplus and China changing from export surplus to import surplus, which resulted in quantities of silver outflow. According to statistics, between 1820 and 1840, China's outflow of silver was around 100 million. The constant outflow of silver caused by the large number of opium imports has begun to disrupt the national treasury and currency circulation of Qing Dynasty, which put Qing's economy on the brink of collapse. More seriously, the spread of opium greatly devastates the physical and mental health of the smokers, and no country can tolerate its development. In June 1839, Qing government appointed the imperial envoy Lin Zexu to destroy opium on Humen beach in Guangdong. With the 23 days from June 3 to 25, 19187 boxes and 2119 bags of opium with a total weight of more than 100 million kilograms were destroyed. Humen, the town near sea in Dongguan, became famous at home and abroad because it turned the page of the modern history of China.

Lin Zexu spent his whole life in fighting against the invasion of foreign enemies. Because of his advocacy of prohibition of opium, in

China, he is regarded as a "national hero".

But he is open to Western culture, technology and trade, advocating learning and using their strengths.

Based on documents, he has at least a slight acquaintance with English and Portuguese and puts efforts to translate Western newspapers, magazines and books.

Wei Yuan, a thinker in late Qing Dynasty, complied the documents translated by Lin Zexu

▲ The Ban-smoking Sculpture. Photogr--apher: Da Guang

and his assistants as *Illustrated Annals of Overseas Countries* from which the Westernization Movement in late Qing Dynasty and even Japan's Meiji Restoration has drawn inspirations.

The event of "Destroying Opium at Humen Beach" makes Dongguan a place where many people have not been to but heard of. However, it is impossible for a city to be respected for only some moments in history. "Dongguan miracles" created since the reform and opening up are known as "a wonderful and vivid miniature of China's reform and opening up", become an advanced model of China's reform and opening up, which is a more important reason of our continuing concentration on this city.

▲ The Ban-smoking Sculpture on Humen Taiping Square.

The Third Plenary Session of the Eleventh Central Committee (its full name is the third plenary session of the Eleventh Central Committee of the Communist Party of China) was held. In *How China Became Capitalist*, Ronald Harry Coase, the winner of the Nobel Prize in Economics and the originator of the new institutional economics, on the road to China's market economy, commented on the conference like this, "a decisive event in the history of the People's Republic; it re-consolidated the power of the Party and paved the way for the reunification of a fractured society. The decisions made there would re-channel the energy, enthusiasm, and creativity of the Chinese people from the politics of class conflict to socialist modernization."

Around this conference, China has gradually implemented a policy of reform and opening up.

In November 1978, Xiaogang Village in Fengyang County, Anhui

Province, began to implement the household contract responsibility system of "parceling out lands to individual households, responsible for one's own profits and losses", which opened the curtain of China's internal reform. In July 1979, Guangdong province and Fujian province were formally approved to carry out special policies and flexible measures in foreign economic activities, and took a historical step of reform and opening up.

Before the reform and opening-up, in Dongguan, the lowest income of a labor is only a few cents. But 30 years later, in 2008, the average annual growth rate of Dongguan economy increased by 18%, creating a high-growth miracle with a faster speed and longer cycle than the early development of "Four Asian Tigers". Dongguan has become one of the fastest growing economies in China. And in terms of comprehensive economic status, it has been on the twelfth position among big and medium-sized cities in China. In fact, the area of Dongguan is not larger or even smaller than many counties in the mainland.

"Asian Four Dragons" in the English world is called "Four Asian Tigers". Dragon is one of the most representative cultural symbols of the Chinese nation. The " Four Asian Tigers" refers to that from the 1960s, Hong Kong, Singapore, South Korea and China Taiwan have implemented the export-oriented strategy focusing on the development of labor-intensive processing industry. Within a short time, Dongguan has achieved the economic take-off, become a developed and rich area in Asia, and been regarded as the representative of the rise of Asian economy. For a long time, the "Four Asian Tigers" became a good example of China, especially the coastal provinces.

On his inspection tour in the south in 1992, Deng Xiaoping put forward that Guangdong should strive to catch up with the "Asian Four Tigers" in 20 years. Dongguan is located in Guangdong province whose economic aggregate has long been 1/7 of the economic aggregate of China. By reference to the national economy in the world, Guangdong is equal to South Korea, ranking twelfth in the world.

Through the development of Guangdong, we can see the development process of Dongguan. Callas, the former chief Asia-Pacific economist of the World Bank, has been quite amazed at " Dongguan miracle" : "Dongguan, known as 'world factory', a city in southern China, which in the past 20 years has maintained an annual growth rate of 20%, within its territory 95% of the needed components for manufacturing and assembling computers are accessible."

Callas also said in his academic report "An East Asian Renaissance: Ideas for Economic Growth" that in 1978, Dongguan was a collection of villages and small towns. The area's population relied primarily on fishing and farming. the Pearl River is only a large town in 1978, its population mainly by fishing and farming for a living. Dongguan today has a population of nearly 7 million. More than 5 million of the inhabitants are migrants who work in the thousands of factories that dot the city, creating a dizzying range of products.

Dongguan Model

What is the secret of Dongguan? Or what is the secret of China's rapid economic development? One and maybe the most important answer is to make use of foreign capital and take the path of developing export-oriented economy.

In July 1978, the State Council (the Central People's Government, the executive organ of the supreme organ of state power in China and the highest administrative organ of the state) issued the *Trial*

Measures for Carrying out Foreign Processing and Assembling Operations. Guangdong, as the leading area and frontier of China's reform and opening up, is the first to make decision of processing materials supplied by clients. By utilizing its own geographical advantages and the advantageous relationship with numerous overseas Chinese, Hong Kong and Macao compatriots, Dongguan began to introduce foreign investment. Due to the shortage of capital, technology and talent, "the three-processing and one compensation" is taken as the starting point of processing trade.

"The three-processing and one compensation" refers to materials processing, sample processing, assembling with provided parts and compensation trade, which is a form of trade tentatively created at the beginning of the reform and opening-up in China. In the framework of "the three-processing and one compensation", the main structure of a company is as follows: foreign clients provide equipment (building factories with foreign investment), raw materials, samples, and are responsible for the export of all products; Chinese enterprises are responsible for providing land, plant and labor. Through the cooperation between Chinese and foreign parties, a new enterprise of " The three-processing and one compensation" is founded.

The first "the three-processing and one compensation" enterprise in the mainland of China, Taiping Handbag Factory was born in Dongguan. This factory, whose predecessor is a Taiping Bamboo Ware House, was set up on September 15, 1978 in Guangdong with an industrial and commercial approval number of YUZI001.

In July 1978, Hong Kong Xinfu Handbag Company with nearly three hundred staff was due to pushed to the brink of collapse due to continuing rising costs. The boss Zhang Zimi came to Humen in Dongguan with a few handbags and some pieces of cloth and found a young man named Tang Zhiping.

▲ The Taiping Handbag Factory with historical meaning.

The 26-year-old Tang Zhiping was responsible for the supply and marketing business in Taiping Garment Factory. Zhang Zimi took out of a black ladies' handbag and some cut-parts of semi-finished handbags, hoping that the

Taiping garment factory could produce such a handbag by imitation as soon as possible.

Once a Chinese media reported such a scene: (Zhang Zimi) took out of a black artificial leather handbag from his bag and asked workers to reproduce a same handbag without any drawings and instructions, which is a problem they had never touched upon. So, three workers who had never seen such a handbag stayed up the whole night to produce a similar handbag with a little raw leather provided by Hong Kong customers and sewing machines. Guests were very satisfied, and a month later they signed a five-year contract with the Second Light Industry Bureau of Guangdong (Taiping Garment Factory was an enterprise below the Second Light Industry Bureau of Guangdong). The first enterprise of "the three-processing and one compensation" was officially unveiled in Dongguan.

Taiping Handbag Factory is located at No. 7 on Jiefang Road in Humen Town, a place where the event of "Destroying Opium at Humen Beach" once took place and again created another No.1 of China. The honorable "YUZI001" went out of business in 1996. However, because of its irreplaceable historical labels, it is often mentioned by Chinse people including the people of Dongguan.

In Dongguan, it became a trend to make use of foreign capital. Enterprises of "the three-processing and one compensation" in Dongguan sprang up like mushrooms.

By the end of 1988, in Dongguan there were more than 2500 enterprises of "the three-processing and one compensation" spreading over

80% of the villages. In 1991, the foreign investment was up to 1.7 billion US dollars. Dongguan has developed from an unknown small agricultural town into a well-known industrial city.

The success of enterprises of "the three-processing and one compensation" has aroused nationwide concern. Such development pattern had also been widely adopted throughout the country. And it has become a nationwide trend to absorb foreign investment to develop economy. A lot of people from coastal areas came to Dongguan to study and learn from Dongguan's successful practice. Some media and economists also stopped in Dongguan and summed up the successful practice into the "Dongguan model" which enjoys a good reputation in China.

The statement that "It doesn't matter whether the cat is black or white, as long as it catches mice." is praised as a theory of the chief designer of China's reform and opening up. This theory expresses a view of proceeding from actual conditions all the time, rather than from rules and regulations. The construction of socialism is realized by actual doing on the consideration of developing social economy, enchaning national comprehensive power and improving people's living standards, instead of talking. This theory has undoubtedly advocated a spirit of working in earnest. The similar widespread statement is "To cross the river by feeling the stones", which also emphasizes the importance of gaining experience from practice. It is precisely because of this, based on practical situations, different places explore different ways of development, and the exploration is summarized as a model.

"Dongguan model" was once the basic model of the implementation of coastal development strategies in China. It is as famous as "Southern Jiangsu model" and "Wenzhou model", each representing different types of economic development model. Coincidentally, these three models take place in the provinces with strong economic strength in China, "Southern Jiangsu model" in Jiangsu Province, "Wenzhou model" in Zhejiang Province.

"Southern Jiangsu model" refers to the way adopted by Jiangsu, Wuxi and Changzhou in southern Jiangsu province to achieve non-agricultural development by developing township enterprises. The main features of the model are as follows: farmers rely on their own strength to develop township enterprises; the pattern of ownership of township enterprises gives priority to collective economy; the township government dominates the development of township enterprises; market regulation is the main means.

Wenzhou people are called Chinese Jews. In the whole country, they are part of those who are most sensitive to the market. They can always capture market opportunities and find the market demand at the earliest. Under the nurture of the market, Wenzhou people spare no effort to develop light manufacturing industry. All of a sudden family workshops are all over the city. Wenzhou people' s small commodities quickly become famous all over the world. The " Wenzhou Model" based on small commodities refers to that, Wenzhou, the southern part of Zhejiang province, develops non-agricultural industries through the cottage industry and professionalized market, as a result of which, the development pattern of small commodities and big market is formed. Small commodities refer to the commodities with small production scale, low technical content and transportation costs. Large market refers to the market network established by Wenzhou people in the whole country.

New development needs even make new demands on government management services. To meet the need of reform and opening up and attracting foreign businesses and investment, Guangdong takes the lead in setting up the country's first processing trade services office, providing one package service for people who start business in Dongguan with all departments working together to solve problems for enterprises and people, which has greatly accelerated the speed of the introduction of foreign investment into Dongguan.

In 2007, with only 0.03% of the national land area, Dongguan created 1.3% of GDP, 1.1% of the fiscal revenue and 4.9% of the total exports, going beyond the economic energy of some provinces in the mainland. So, the outside world uses "richer than a province" to describe the economic capacity of Dongguan.

It is in the process of economic development, Dongguan rapidly while quietly conducts urbanization and develops from an agricultural county to an industrial big city. Around 1990, the booming scene of "village fire, household smoke" could be seen everywhere in the rural areas of Dongguan. Some people summarized such urbanization as "rural urbanization of urban-rural integration".

China's urbanization rate reached 57.35% in 2016. Figures show that by 2020, China's urbanization rate will reach 60%. In 1978, this figure was only 17.9%. Urbanization is the process of human progress must go through, through the urbanization, marking the realization of the goal of modernization.

In 1984, the reform and development of the rural areas in China was still in the stage of perfecting the household contract responsibility system. However, Dongguan had already completed rural economic management system and started to change to the commodity agriculture. Due to the rapid development of the township enterprises, the labor force was accelerated to change to the non-agricultural industry. So, in that year, Dongguan put forward the goal of "marching into rural industrialization".

Rural industrialization has promoted the process of urban-rural integration and urbanization. In 1992, Dongguan established the strategy of "building Dongguan in accordance with the modern urban structure", which soon makes Dongguan from the original rural town into the group city with characteristics of urban-rural integration. Since 2001, Dongguan has set off a new upsurge of urban construction.

Like many developing cities in China, the visual boundaries of the city and the countryside are no longer so clear, and in countryside too many western-style buildings have been built. In recent years, it has been popular for urban people to travel and live in rural areas. However, 30 years ago, it is the very countryside where they want to leave.

Benefiting from the rapid economic development, Dongguan took the lead in the implementation of agricultural tax exemption, popularizing high school education, exempting urban and rural students from tuition and incidental fees as well as textbooks fees at the stage of compulsory education in Guangdong. Dongguan also took the lead in implementing the farmer (town dweller) endowment insurance, the farmer (town dweller) basic medical insurance as well as endowment insurance designed for family planning.

Some people think that this path represents the direction of the urbanization and modernization of Chinese rural areas. The research office of the General Office of the CPC Central Committee once pointed out: " Dongguan Road has provided a realistic and feasible model of urbanization in China", and will "provide some important inspirations for China's modernization".

"The Traffic Jam in Dongguan, the Stockout in the World"

Things are constantly changing, some in the right direction.

Despite of the amazing development achievements achieved in the 1980s, Dongguan does not lie on its laurels and constantly looks for new opportunities. At that time, Dongguan basically developed labor-intensive industries with low technical content and low added value, mainly relied on the increase in foreign labor to support economic growth, which is an extensive method of economic growth.

With the entry of more and more IT companies and the formation of IT communities, Dongguan' s economy has undergone profound changes. The total exports of Dongguan increased from US $39 million in 1978 to US $ 60.232 billion in 2007, with an increase of 1543.4 times and an average annual growth rate of 27.7%. Dongguan became the city with the third highest export volume after Shenzhen and Shanghai, and ranked first among prefecture-level cities.

There are two sayings, that is, "If Dongguan is in traffic jam, the world will be out of stock." and "If Dongguan is in traffic jam, the world will have a cold.". Because here the production of computer motherboards, magnetic heads and drives accounts for more than 75% of the total production in the world. "No matter where you place orders, the place of production is Dongguan." It is a fact that Dongguan has become a modern manufacturing city.

Dongguan needs to and must achieve the transformation and upgrading of industrial structure and transform into a more advanced mode of economic development. In 1994, Dongguan announced that Dongguan had basically achieved the industrialization of the countryside, which is the end of Dongguan's "First Industrial Revolution", and the next step is to seize the opportunity in good time to promote the "Second Industrial Revolution."

"Second Industrial Revolution" refers to the rapid transformation of labor-intensive industries into technology-intensive industries and the slow transformation of "quantitative" economy into "quality" economy, whose

▲ Dongguan Songshan Lake High-tech Development Zone has become the banner of independent innovation in Dongguan.

proposal and implementation marks the beginning of upgrade and transformation of Dongguan economy.

Dongguan has seized rare opportunities and undertaken the second wave of international industry transfer. At that time, the advanced IT industry developed rapidly in Dongguan. Known as the "IT capital in China", Dongguan held the E-business Expo which became one of the four major international computer information Expos. Dongguan is the largest computer components manufacturing base in the world. 95% of the computer components are produced in Dongguan.

Within more than 30 years, starting from the way of "the three-processing and one compensation", the industrial level of the export-oriented economy of Dongguan is continually rising and the product connotation is continually upgrading. Into the 1980s, Dongguan mainly undertook traditional manufacturing industry with small business scale and low additional value, such as Hong Kong textile, shoemaking, bag and luggage making and toymaking. Into the 1990s, the IT manufacturing industry based on computer peripheral products from Taiwan, Japan and South Korea flooded into Dongguan, so Dongguan became a manufacturing capital.

Of course, IT mannfactuning industry is far from enough. Dongguan finally formed a manufacturing system with complete range, perfect facilities and advanced technology, covering more than 30 industries and more than 60,000 kinds of products. Most industrial products in the world can find their supporting industry and products in the "industrial biologic chain" of Dongguan enterprise groups. In a sense, Dongguan is the sample region of "MADE IN CHINA". In Dongguan, you can always find a sample to analyze any sign of disturbance or trouble about the manufacturing industry. Dongguan has become a "foundry" for various types of manufacturing of electronic information, electrical machinery and equipment, textile, footwear and headwear, food and beverage, paper and paper products.

Dongguan is also a capital of shoes, clothing and toys. One of every ten pairs of shoes in the world are manufactured in Dongguan. It is still a " Capital of Garments" . In Dalang Town in Guangdong, a place where there are almost no seasonal changes, someone can still wear short-sleeved T-shirts in December and a place does not produce any wool. Annually it sells more than 10 billion pieces of sweater, which means that in every five people in the world there is a man who wear a sweater produced in Dalang Town.

Jiangmen:
Still a Door to Sea

The "Hometown of Overseas Chinese" with Outstanding People and Smart Land

After we finished dinner at Chen's little school, the heat of the day had already diminished. The sun retreated behind the hills, leaving brightly colored clouds hanging in the sky, over the hills and trees.

We walked through a gravel path, and before long we reached the bank, where a pavilion stood made of straw. Filing through the pavilion, we found several small boats anchored under two big trees along the bank.

One after another, we hopped into one of the boats. One friend loosened the rope, pushed the bamboo pole against the bank, which moved the boat to the center of the river.

The river was wide, the water glistening without a ripple. The boat was steadily floating on the water, the three oars pulling in rhythm.

Then the river narrowed at a certain point. Clusters of leaves stretched out touching the water's surface. The leaves were in a lovely green color. There seemed to be many lush banyan trees, but I couldn't make out where the main trunks of the trees were.

My friends immediately corrected me as I referred to them as being many banyan trees. One of them said it was only one banyan, and another said there were two. I had seen many enormous banyans before, but it was the first time I saw such a gigantic one.

As the boat drew nearer to the banyan, I finally got a good look at it. This was a huge tree, with countless branches, on which grew aerial prop roots. Many of the roots were dangling to the ground, some all the way into the soil. There were branches hanging above the water. Seen from a distance, the tree seemed to be reposed on the water.

It was in the lush season. The banyan seemed to showcase its vibrant life energy to us. There were many leaves, clusters over clusters, with not even a tiny hole existing. The emerald green shining brightly in front of our eyes, it was like on each leaf there was a new life dancing. What a tree it is growing in the beautiful southern part of China!

The boat was moored under the tree for a moment, but we didn't get onto the bank because it was so wet. A friend said it was known as the "paradise of the birds" here. The local peasants forbade anyone to catch these birds. I thought I had heard some sounds of flapping wings, but by the time I shifted my eyes to that direction, I didn't see any birds. There were many roots sticking out on the ground, looking like stakes. The soil was wet, perhaps for the tides frequently washed onto the shore. There were no birds in the "paradise of the birds," I thought. The boat moved again, as a friend pushed the boat, and it drifted to the center of the river.

On the following day, we boated to a friend's hometown, the place we had seen the hills and the pagoda. Setting off from a little school, we passed the "paradise of the birds" again.

This time it was morning, and the sun was pouring over the water, as well as the branches. Everything was extremely bright. We stopped under the tree for a moment.

It was very quiet at first, but then a burst of chirps broke the silence. We clapped our hands, and saw a big bird flying over, then a second, and a third. We continued to clap, and soon the woods became very boisterous. Bird chirps

▲ A Paradise of Birds in Xinhui District in Jiangmen City.

were all over the place, and so were the birds, the big ones, small ones, variegated ones and black ones. Some perched on the branches, chirping; some were flying up; some were flapping their wings.

I busied myself by watching them. Just as I saw this one clearly, I already missed the other one, and when I turned my eyes to the second one, the third one had flown off. A thrush flew out, but was startled by our clapping and then turned back into the woods. It stopped at a thin branch, and started to sing enthusiastically. The sounds were so beautiful.

As the boat was floating to the village under the pagoda, I kept turning back to look at the lush banyan left behind. I felt a little melancholy to leave this place. Yesterday, I was cheated by my eyes. The "paradise of the birds" is a real paradise for the birds!

---Ba Jin *The Paradise of Birds*

In 1933, one of the most famous writer in modern China, Ba Jin went sightseeing on the sandbank in the middle of Tianma River in Xinhui Area of Jiangmen City. There was a banyan with a history of more than 500 years on the islet. The branches of this tree dangled to the ground, some all the way into the soil, and became new roots. As time went on, the big banyan has grown into a forest in which thousands of birds inhabited. Ba Jin had some thoughts on such scenery and wrote down the essay — *The Paradise of Birds* which has been chosen into Chinese textbook for primary schools and become the spiritual memory of several generations of Chinese people.

49 years later, in 1982, Ba Jin again personally named this scenic spot "The Birds of Paradise". Since then, this name has been widely broadcasted in the world. Today, this place has already been the largest natural bird-watching park in the country and the famous international eco-attraction in Xinhui District.

Birds' paradise is the portrayal of the characteristics of Jiangmen. The birds suddenly appear and disappear but will not fly away from the sandbar, so do people.

Jiangmen is located at the confluence of the Xijiang River and its tributary Pengjiang River. Penglai Mountain and Yandun Mountain face each other like a door respectively on the northern and southern side of the Pengjiang River, thus "Jiangmen" is given the name.

Since ancient times Jiangmen has been the land of talents. "One family nourishes three academicians, and nine children are all talented". The nine children of the famous modern thinker Liang Qichao from

Xinhui District in Jiangmen all become successful and have their own strengths.

Liang Qichao is recognized as an outstanding scholar in the late Qing Dynasty, an encyclopedia-type person in Chinese history. Before the Revolution of 1911 which ends the rule of Qing Dynasty, in the debate with revolutionaries, he invented a new literary style, a style between the ancient Chinese and modern vernacular Chinese. Because it is easy to understand and flexible in syntax, it is very popular among people. Liang Qichao is the first person in China to use the term "Chinese nation" in articles.

There is one thing about him which is most known to Chinese people. In 1895, he, along with thousands of successful candidates in imperial examinations at the provincial level, submitted a joint letter to the Emperor Guangxu to fight against signing the "Treaty of Shimonoseki" which humiliates the country and forfeits its sovereignty after failing the Sino-Japanese War. This event is known as "Gongche Shangshu movement". Subsequently, supported by the emperor, he and his teacher Kang Youwei launched the Hundred Days Reform to advocate science and culture, reform political and educational system and develop agriculture, industry, business.

More than 100 days later, the movement failed, and most of the new policies were canceled. But the first national university in modern China, Imperial University of Peking, was kept. In 1912, Imperial University of Peking changed its name to Peking University. Peking University has always been one of the best universities in China.

Jiangmen locates in the western part of the Pearl River Delta. The five districts including Xinhui District (city), Kaiping County, Taishan County, Enping County and Heshan County under Jiangmen are well-known as "Wuyi" (the five counties) inside and outside the country, because the culture and customs of these five places are basically the same. In Jiangmen there are nearly 4 million overseas Chinese, ethnic Chinese, compatriots in Hong Kong and Macau, distributing over 107 countries and regions in five continents, 20% in Asia and 70% in the Americas.

In China, most famous hometowns of overseas Chinese are Jiangmen, Quanzhou, Chaoshan, Meizhou. Most of overseas Chinese from Quanzhou, Chaoshan and Meizhou are in Southeast Asia. Only overseas Chinese from Wuyi (five counties) are mainly distributed in the United States, Canada and Australia. It creates opportunities for Wuyi to promote cultural communications between China and foreign countries, in the meantime, preserves traditional Chinese culture. Traces of Sino- West blend can be found everywhere, from architecture, catering, clothing to customs.

Situ Meitang is one of them.

On April 3, 1868, he was born in a farmer's family in Chikan Town, Kaiping County, Guangdong Province. In March

▲ One representative of overseas Chinese-Situ Meitang.

1880, only at the age of 12, Situ Meitang walked to Hong Kong from Kaiping and alone sailed to the United States by ferry.

In 1894, Situ Meitang came to Boston and set up On Leong Tong, advocating "fight for the weak against the strong, suppress the evil and pacify the good". On Leong Tong soon became a strong group owned by Chinese Freemasons, and finally spread over 31 cities in the United States, with large scale and more than 20,000 members. In 1905, Situ Meitang set up the general hall of On Leong Tong in New York, and the legal adviser was the later US president — Franklin Roosevelt.

Then Situ Meitang met Sun Yat-sen. When Sun Yat-sen launched movements in the United States, for protecting Sun Yat-sen, Situ Meitang accompanied him as a fulltime bodyguard and chef. In April 1911, after the Second Guangzhou Uprising failed, Tung Meng Hui was badly in need of 150,000 US dollars. Situ Meitang encouraged his fellows in Chinese Freemasons to donate. But he knew well that it was hard to collect such a huge amount of money in a short time merely relying on donation of overseas Chinese. In desperation, he put the four buildings of Chinese Freemasons in Toronto, Vancouver, Victoria and Jinshan Building in pawn. And later he sold a few buildings of Chinese Freemasons, scraped up the 150,000 US dollars, and supported armed uprisings. After the Wuchang Uprising took place in the same year, when Sun Yat-sen went back home from the United States, his travelling expenses were paid by Situ Meitang and others.

In 1932, the January 28 Incident broke out. The general Cai Tingkai led soldiers in the Nineteenth Route Army to bravely resist Japanese invaders. After news spread to the United States, Situ Meitang immediately organized donations and returned to the motherland with donations to comfort soldiers. He and Cai Tingkai also became close friends.

"Qiao" (overseas Chinese) is the"NDA"of Jiangmen city and the essential difference from other cities. Beginning in 2015, Jiangmen officially launched the construction of the capital of overseas Chinese, putting forward the need to polish the card of the capital of overseas China. Jiangmen also introduced the implemented the plan and action program for overseas Chinese business and city construction. At the end of 2016, Jiangmen put forward the requirement to vigorously develop global tourism, to build a strong tourism city, and to set up a special international travel destination in China. Kaiping City and Taishan City were confirmed as one of the units of national tourism demonstration areas.

The long "Chaoren Path" in the capital of overseas Chinese has become an important tool for the development of overseas Chinese affairs and tourism. "Chaoren Path" advocates measuring the prosper of the city by foot, connecting the existing roads, village roads, forest roads, climbing trails, country roads and other lines in series with nature protection areas, scenic spots, historical sites, ancient villages and rural scenery to form an urban and rural slow walking system, with characteristics of the hometown of overseas Chinese. In 2017, Jiangmen will construct the "Chaoren Path" with a total length of 3,000 kilometers. Over a period of time, "Chaoren Path" strives for a total length of 10,000 kilometers to create "the First Walking Path in Guangdong".

Centurial Diaolou
and Overseas Chinese's Town

There is an old man whose family name is "Guan" in Chikan Town, Kaiping County. More than 30 of his relatives live in the United States and Canada. In Kaiping, the hometown of overseas Chinese, families like him can be found everywhere. It is said that Kaiping has a population of 650,000 people and 750,000 overseas relatives.

The famous Diaolou (the fortified multi-story tower) has recorded the rise and fall of a family of overseas Chinese, and maintained the love for the hometown and country rooted in the local and extended to the rest of the world. From gold mining and railway construction in North American, to the later rubber tapping and manor running in Southeast Asia, to the present emigration, Diaolou has witnessed stories of generation after generation who made a long and difficult journey to realize their dreams.

The architecture in the hometown of overseas Chinese in Wuyi fully integrates with the characteristics of Western architecture, among which, Kaiping Diaolou is the most famous and most special one. Kaiping Diaolou, combining traditional Chinese architectural culture with the uniqueness of Western architectural culture, has become a monument to the memory of overseas Chinese culture and reflected the course of overseas Chinese and Chinese people's initiative acceptance of Western culture.

The amount of Kaiping Diaolou is more than 1,800. In 2007,

▲ Jiangmen Diaolou. Photographer: Chen Jie

"Kaiping Diaolou and Villages" was officially listed on the World Heritage List, becoming the 35th world heritage in China. Thus, the first world heritage project of overseas Chinese culture was born in China.

World Heritage Committee evaluates Guangdong Kaiping Diaolou like this: Kaiping Diaolou are multi-storeyed defensive village houses in Kaiping. Retaining a harmonious relationship with the surrounding landscape, Kaiping Diaolou display a complex and flamboyant fusion of Chinese and Western structural and decorative forms.

After Ming Dynasty, in Jiangmen area, bandits were rampant and social security was in chaos. Additionally, there were many rivers in this area. When there were typhoon rainstorms, flood disaster frequently occurred. Clever Jiangmen people chose to build fortified multi-story towers in the village for protection.

In the 1920s, Diaolou ushered in the peak period of its construction. Overseas Chinese who had lived abroad for decades returned home with their savings and built multi-storeyed defensive towers one after another to protect their families and properties.

Kaiping Diaolou are multi-storeyed buildings, higher than ordinary houses, which makes it convenient for condescending defense. Walls of the towers are thicker than the ordinary houses. So, residents in Kaiping are not afraid of robbers' chiseling holes in the walls or fire attack. The towers have smaller windows than the ordinary houses. Many windows are equipped with iron gratings and sashes as well as iron plates outwards. The upper four corners of towers are generally equipped with total-closed or semi-closed hornworks (commonly known as "swallow nests") which reach out of cantilevers. Inside every hornwork there are forward and downward shooting holes, through which you can shoot at village invaders in a higher position. At the same time, on each wall of every story there are shooting holes, increasing the number of attack points for residents.

Kaiping Diaolou have different usages, resulting in different classifications: the public tower, the living tower and the watchtower.

Villagers or some families raise money to build living towers at the back of the village. One family gets one room to avoid bandits or floods. Living towers are also built at the back of the village by wealthy people. With large space and fully equipped living facilities, living towers have two functions: defense and living. Watchtowers are mainly built at the gate of the village or hills and riversides outside the village. Many watchtowers are equipped with searchlights and alarms, which makes it easy for villagers to find out bandits in advance and warn villagers in other villages.

The upper part of Kaiping Diaolou is most expressive. People mainly make use of the dome, mountain flower, order and other architectural elements which appear in foreign buildings, forming thousands of architectural styles. Different architectural styles reflect the different economic strength of the landlord, aesthetic taste and the extent of the impact of foreign architectural culture.

The Diaolou cluster located in Zili Village, Tangkou Town, Kaiping County is one of the world cultural heritage sites. It became famous because it is the place where Chinese film *Let the Bullets Fly* was shot.

Let the Bullets Fly is a film released in 2010 and set in in southern China during the warring 1920s. After ambushing a government horse train, the leading bandit Zhang Muzhi came across a big liar Lao Tang. They develop from enemies to close friends. However, the real battle has just begun. Huang Silang, the mobster boss in southern China, casts greedy eyes on Goose Town. A series of breathtaking battles are put on stage one after another.

In 2017, the total number of Chinese cinema screens has been more than 40,000. China has become a country with most cinema screens in the world. Chinese movies seem to usher in the best of times, but real impressive movies are rare. The film *Let the Bullets Fly* is considered as one

▲ In Zili Village, there are 15 towers with different styles, delicate shapes and rich connotations, which are outstanding representatives of Kaiping Diaolou in the flourishing period. Photographer: Chen Jie

of the films worth recording in this era.

Let the Bullets Fly is directed and starred by Jiang Wen, one of the most important figures in contemporary Chinese film industry. It is his fourth film.

Yunhuan Tower is one of the 15 towers in Zili Village. In 1921, Yunhuan Tower was built with an area of 80 square meters.

This year, China was still seeking an independent and prosperous road. For Chinese people, this year the most important thing is that the first national congress of the Communist Party of China was held in Shanghai and the Communist Party of China was born. 28 years later, the Chinese Communist Party became China's ruling party and founded the People's Republic of China.

The constructor of Huanyun Tower Fang Wenxian had lived in

Malaysia and was enthusiastic about public welfare. In 1918, Fang Wenxian donated 5000 yuan and raised 17000 yuan for building Qiangya School in his hometown. During Japanese invasion of China, he donated money for the resistance against Japanese invasion and purchased liberty bonds.

He built this tower out of consideration of reverting to his origin. The external style and decoration of the five-storied Yunhuan Tower has some characteristics of the Western style. But inside the tower, Fang Wenxian' and his families' living utensils are still preserved, showing an image of traditional rural home furnishings in southern China.

He also personally wrote a couplet for the tower:「雲龍風虎際會常懷怎奈壯志莫愁只贏得湖海生涯空山歲月 幻影曇花身世如夢何妨豪情自放無負此陽春煙景大塊文章」.

The couplet is expressed that: they often have a big career desire, but unfortunately the ambition is difficult to achieve, can only wander rivers and lakes, helpless wasted years; although everything is like phantom, there is still a need to express lofty sentiments to live up to the present beautiful spring scenery and splendid articles.

In Chinese culture, a couplet should have a horizontal scroll. The horizontal scroll of the couplet is "only talking about personal sentiments". The businessman present his love for his country and his hometown as well as his resentment and depression towards turbulent times in the couplet.

Not only towers, in Kaiping country, there are some villages whose name is deeply marked with the " Qiao" (overseas Chinese). The emergence and construction of these villages is a miniature of the immigrant history of

▲ Canadian Village. Photographer: Chen Jie

hometowns of overseas Chinese, behind which is written the struggling entrepreneurial spirit as well as patriotic feeling of overseas Chinese.

Speaking of buildings overseas Chinese villages, people will be surprised with constructors' particular selection of building materials. Some of building materials needed to build luxury houses were directly purchased overseas. "Canadian Village" was designed by hiring Canadian designers who brought the construction drawings of villages and villas back home, and with the combination of Chinese and Western cultural elements. The steels, cement and wood needed to construct villas were also shipped from Canada to Hong Kong and then to Kaiping by Canadian overseas Chinese, which took three months.

Walking into the "Burmese Village", you will see 12 two-storied high houses arranged in two rows, neatly located in the fields. In front of the village is the open ground, and outside the village is the pond. The distance between houses are "equidistant", about 2 meters wide. The roofs are the hard summit-type structure of pad surface; walls are built up with black bricks; stairs and doors are made teakwood; beams are shaped like the Chinese character "Gong" and built with iron and teakwood.

Most of these houses are with two rooms, two corridors and one hall, and a few houses are with one room and one gallery. The needed teakwood is purchased from Burma; cement and steel is transported back from Hong Kong by hiring ships. The constructor of the village is Xu Suixing. To make a living, he went to Burma with his brother Xu Chunxing, and did odds and ends in a wood factory. Because of working hard, a few years later, they had a certain savings, and set up a wood factory named "Wang Xing Long". In its heyday, the shops run by him are up to dozens. He became a well-known local businessman. Although their days in Burma were quite comfortable, the two still inevitably missed their home, so they afterwards returned home to build houses.

Sprouted Overseas, Rooted in Jiangmen

"Dad goes to San Francisco, soon send money back, the whole family rely on you, to send money back." This is a ballad familiarized by overseas Chinese whose ancestral home is in Jiangmen. In old China, a lot of Chinese people were abducted to labor in foreign countries as "piglets". They travelled far away across the sea to San Francisco in the United States, and then washed mineral sands, did hard manual work and participated in the construction of the US Central Pacific Railway. 80% of the Chinese railway constructors came from Jiangmen. Too many people passed away in a foreign country.

An article entitled *Overseas Chinese Deep Love for Jiangmen* introduces that when Sun Yat-sen led the Revolution of 1911, established "Revive China Society", "Tung Meng Hui" and the KMT, Jiangmen overseas Chinese enthusiastically participated. Sun Yat-sen organized armed uprisings 10 times, and funds needed were afforded by overseas Chinese, among whom Jiangmen overseas Chinese made the greatest contributions. He once said that " overseas Chinese as the mother of revolution", which indicates overseas Chinese great contributions to the revolution.

From 1937 to August 1945, Jiangmen overseas Chinese donations in the United States reached more than 56 million US dollars. At that time the National Government issued nation-saving government bonds six times

▲ Jiangmen Wuyi Overseas Chinese Museum intensively displays historical culture, customs, economic development, social progress and folk art of the hometown of overseas Chinese, including the literature and relics about the migration of overseas Chinese as well as various kinds of typical working tools and living appliances once used by overseas Chinese at home and abroad, and some of them are of great value. The picture is a statue in the museum, showing that Chinese labors are constructing the American Western Railway. Photographer: Chen Jie

with a total value of 3 billion yuan, of which Jiangmen overseas Chinese subscribed for 1.11 billion yuan.

In 2010, Jiangmen Wuyi Overseas Chinese Museum was fully open to the public. More than 40,000 pieces of collections of overseas Chinese in the museum faithfully and fully record this phase of history, tell touching stories about Wuyi overseas Chinese who start their business abroad and make contributions to their hometown.

Chen Yixi, a villager in Meitang Village, Liu Village, Doushan Town, Taishan City, born in 1844, went to America at the age of 11, then participated in the US railway construction and became a railway engineer. And then he was engaged in business, running operating "Guang De Hao", participated in many construction projects in Seattle and became an influential Chinese businessman. During the period of US exclusion of Chinese, Chen Yixi defied brutal suppression, actively fought for Chinese rights and interests as well as united and organized people to resist against suppressions. He was admired and loved by overseas Chinese, becoming an influential leader of overseas Chinese.

At the age of 60, Chen Yuxi gave up superior living conditions in the United States, came back his poor hometown, led the villagers to build a railway of Chinese people—Sunning Railway. The construction of Sunning Railway was without any participation of foreign loans, foreign stocks and foreign workers. It was constructed on Chinese own, from the preparation, design, construction, operation to management, which set a new trend. He was determined to "construct a railway of Chinese own by using Chinese capital, to make outstanding achievements by virtue of Chinese strength".

The construction of Sunning railway was officially started on May 1, 1906 and completed on March 30, 1920, which lasts 14 years. The railway has a total length of 133 kilometers and includes 46 stations, 215 bridges and 236 culverts. In addition, a large number of projects such as Gongyi Terminal, Beijie Terminal, Gongyi Machine Factory and Niuwan Shipping Company were completed one after another. What's more, "turntables" and "train ferries" are pioneering achievements in Chinese railroad history, establishing a land and water transport network with Taicheng as a transportation hub and Sunning Railway as the main line. This transport network has become the main artery of the social and economic development of Jiangmen Wuyi in the Republic of China era.

In 1933, Bajin took a train ferry on Sunning railway passing through the Tangjiang River and wrote down the famous prose "The Poem of Machine".

He wrote: "In order to see a friend, I became a passenger on Sunning Railway. My three friends and I spent about three hours on the train all the way from Huicheng to Gongyi. Despite of long time and hot weather, I did not feel lonely.

The scenery in the South was indeed enchanting. In my eyes, everything was beautiful like a dream: lush green trees, bright red soil, pieces of rice fields, piles of houses, the mirror-like river and lofty towers. Although the countryside in the South contained a lot of pain, on the surface they were still very calm and very beautiful! Arriving Tanjiang, the train stopped. The wheels did not move; however, the outside scenery began to move slowly. This is not a miracle. This is the most beautiful project on the Sunning Railway. "

Sunning Railway has been run around for 30 years. During the AntiJapanese War, it was severely damaged by Japanese troops, then the National Government ordered to demolish it, and only the site of Beijing Railway Station was left until now.

Based on data, overseas Chinese, ethnic Chinese as well as Hong Kong, Macao and Taiwan compatriots whose ancestral home are Jiangmen are nearly 4 million, spreading all over 107 countries and regions in the world. The population of overseas Chinese and ethnic Chinese is the basically equal with the population of Jiangmen City. So, there is a saying about Jiangmen: "two Jiangmen respectively at home and abroad".

Political figures, such as the former American Ambassador to China Gary Faye Locke, the Mayor of San Francisco Edwin Mah Lee, the Mayor of Auckland City Jean Quan, the Chief Executive of the Macao Special Administrative Region Fernando Chui as well as Hong Kong stars such as Andy Lau, Chow Yun Fat, Alan Tam, Tony Leung and Donnie Yen are all rooted in Jiangmen.

Overseas Chinese love their country and hometown. They make contributions to the development of their hometown by means of donation and investment. By the end of 2015, their donations for their hometown were up to 7.26 billion Hong Kong dollars, and the investment amounted to 20.22 billion US dollars. Jiangmen specially set up the " honorary citizen" award system to commend overseas Chinese, foreigners and domestic people who have made outstanding contributions in promoting the civilized development of charitable and public service, friendly foreign exchanges as well as economic and technological development in Jiangmen. Since 1993, eight batches of 700 people at home and abroad have been dubbed "Honorary Citizens of Jiangmen City".

Huang Xiaojuan is an honorary citizen of Jiangmen City. She grew up in Sabah, Malaysia, and studied in Canada in her early years. After graduating from college, she followed his father to do real estate business, and step by step became a famous female entrepreneur in Sabah.

Huang Xiaojuan's father has donated more than 100 million yuan for the reconstruction of playgrounds and teaching buildings in local schools in Taishan. Huang Xiaojuan remembers that since 1980, her father has returned home every year to visit relatives. In 1998, Huang Xiaojuan paid her first visit to Taishan, and after hearing that some primary schools need to be repaired, she immediately contacted with these schools.

For Huang Xiaojuan, it is a kind of honor and responsibility to become a bridge linking together the economy , trade and culture of Jiangmen and Sabah.

Outstanding overseas Chinese with family ties in Jiangmen should also include Julie Fong. At the 36th Grammy Awards in 1994, by virtue of Ten Summoner's Tales, Julie Fong won the trophy of the best music production. This is the first time for a Chinese to stand on the podium of the Grammy Award.

Born in 1964 in San Francisco, Julie Fong, whose ancestral home is in Shangtang Village, Qiangya Village Committee, Tangkou Town, Kaiping City, Guangdong Province, is the second generation of Chinese. Her father Fang Chuangjie is a well-known overseas Chinese leader. In the 1950s, he founded an insurance bank named after his own name in San Francisco. In university Julie Fong tried film and television production, and after graduation she produced music videos.

In recognition of Julie Fong's achievements, on July 16, 1994, in addition to the award, the Mayor's office of San Francisco declared the day of 16th as "Julie Fong Day".

廣州：
古港新作為

黃埔古港的前世今生

二〇一五年十二月，廣東省會廣州，這個一千三百多萬人口的大都市，正在廣州博物館舉行「哥德堡號」瓷器展覽。這近百件瓷器出發於一七四五年的廣州，卻在瑞典的哥德堡（Goteborg）港海底沉睡二百多年。用中國人的話說，它這算是「回娘家」。

一七四五年一月十一日，瑞典商船「哥德堡號」從廣州啟程回國，船上裝載著大約七百噸在廣州採購的中國貨物，包括三百六十六噸茶葉、五十萬到七十萬件瓷器，還有絲綢、藤器和珍珠母等。這是它第三次來廣州，也是最後一次。

一七五七年清朝政府宣布實行「一口通商」，各國來中國貿易都要來到廣州，也只能來到廣州。

這一年，按中國的舊曆是清乾隆二十二年。乾隆是當時中國最高統治者愛新覺羅・弘曆皇帝的年號。中國古代新皇登基，為了區別前任（多數是自己的父親），會設置一個年號，用於計算年份。乾隆二十二年就是弘曆當上皇帝的第二十二個年頭。

乾隆，寓意「天道昌隆」，事實也正如此。乾隆是中國古代壽命最長的一個皇帝，他活了八十八歲。從他的爺爺康熙皇帝（這位是最受中國人欣賞的古代最高統治者之一），到他的父親雍正皇帝，再到乾隆皇帝，是中國歷史上文化、經濟、手工業極盛的時代。在中國，對一個朝代最大的褒獎就是被稱為盛世──在很長時間內保持繁榮昌盛──這三位皇帝締造了中國的「康乾盛世」。

「康乾盛世」中「乾」字所代表的皇帝就是乾隆。乾隆自稱

「十全老人」，「十全」表示沒有欠缺，可見這位皇上的自信。他還是中國寫過最多古詩的人，據說是三萬多首，即使唐宋詩詞巔峰時的那些偉大詩人也無法與他相比。

「一口通商」三十五年後，一七九二年英國派馬嘎爾尼率船隊以為乾隆補祝八十大壽的名義來到了中國，按規定藩屬國見皇帝都要下跪，雙方在是否下跪以及怎樣下跪上進行了事關尊嚴和國體但實際上更是文化隔閡的爭議。後世的人會認為，這實際上是中國從開放走向封閉的象徵。

航行八個月後，「哥德堡號」來到離哥德堡港大約九百米的海面，離家三十個月的船員們已能看到自己的故鄉，然而就在這個時候，船頭觸礁隨即沉沒，正在岸上等待凱旋的人們只好眼睜睜地目睹船沉到海裡。幸運的是，所有船員安然無恙。

大約三分之一的貨物被打撈出來，在市場上出售所得除了支付這次廣州之旅的全部成本外，竟然還能獲利百分之十四。「哥德堡號」和船上三分之二的貨物長眠海底，默默等待著二百多年後重見天日的那一刻。一九八四年，瑞典一次民間考古活動發現了「哥德堡號」殘骸。兩年後，開始考古發掘。很快，就打撈出四百多件完整的瓷器和九噸重的瓷器碎片，這些瓷器大部分具有中國傳統的圖案花紋，少量繪有歐洲特色圖案，顯然是當年「哥德堡號」為特定客戶專門訂購的「訂燒瓷」。

當「哥德堡號」再次來到廣州時，已是一百五十年後的二〇〇九年。不過，這次是仿製舊船而造的新船，按照中國人的習慣，稱它為「哥德堡三號」。

它耗費了四千名工匠的十年時間，當然還有三千萬美元。

廣州為迎接這位「新朋友」，斥巨資在黃埔古港和南海神廟重建了兩個碼頭，碼頭及其周邊都以古代樣式為藍本，復原二百多年前的景象。他們希望展示以海上絲綢之路為代表的中國海洋文化，展現廣州的貿易歷史，再塑千年古港的世界聲譽。

　　「哥德堡三號」航行路線也按古時安排，這是十六世紀前全世界最長的一條航線。一切很順利，但到達廣州花了它三百多天的時間，航程約為三千七百公里。

　　瑞典國王卡爾十六世古斯塔夫和西爾維亞王后同船抵達。據說，把廣州選為「哥德堡三號」到中國後的第一個城市，是國王本人的要求。廣州人沒有辜負瑞典人的厚誼，參觀者絡繹不絕。

　　新銳雜誌《新週刊》這樣評價「哥德堡三號」來到廣州：兩個國家的兩座城市，用一艘仿古帆船，一條古代商貿航線，上演了一場有二百多年歷史內涵的好戲。中央電視台把這個創舉錄進了《探索與發現》欄目，廣州人把它視為「花多少錢也買不來的宣傳廣州的大好機會」，瑞典人把復航計劃變成一次極具創意的「文化形象工程」。「哥德堡號」的重生，展示了一個值得借鑑的公關模式，它既是贊助商的市場公關，也是國家的經貿公關，更是民族的文化公關。

　　「哥德堡三號」連接的是廣州對外交往的歷史與未來。到廣州後，它還是像一八五七年那樣，停泊在黃埔古港——一個一千五百年從未與外界失去聯繫，即便在清末閉關鎖國時依舊頑強生存的「一口通商」之地。

　　「凡載洋貨入口之外國商船，不得沿江灣泊，必須下錨於黃埔」。黃埔，就是黃埔古港。從一七五八年至一八三七年的八十年間，停泊在黃埔古港的外國商船共計五千一百零七艘。作為相當長一段時間內中國唯一的港口，它見證了廣州「海上絲綢之路」的繁榮，迎接了包括美國的「中國皇后號」、俄羅斯的「希望號」等外國商船，特別是「中國皇后號」的訪華，打開了中美貿易的大門。

中國歷史學家黃仁宇在其著作《萬曆十五年》中，從大歷史的角度提出中國在近代化的過程中落後，無關道德和個人因素，而是在技術上不能實現「數目字管理」。但在有些數字上，其實中國人做得不錯，比如關於這五千一百零七艘船的統計。

在中國偉大的史學家、文學家、思想家司馬遷筆下，廣州是「珠璣、犀、瑇瑁、果、布之湊」的大都會。黃埔古港位於現在的廣州市海珠區新港東路。它所在的黃埔村，仍是一派古樸景色。渡口旁的大榕樹斜橫，芭蕉林悅眼，漁船點點，不過已鮮見商貿的痕跡。

黃埔村原村名為「鳳浦」，村南緊靠珠江就有一座刻有「鳳浦」二字的綵牌坊。相傳古時有一對鳳凰飛臨此地，從此人丁興旺，五穀豐登。傳說終歸會是美好而吉祥的。

該村地處一小島，在中國水邊地區叫「浦」，水中的陸地曰「洲」，所以取村名為「凰洲」或「鳳浦」，後演變成為「黃埔」之名。

村中保留的大量遺跡和文物，見證了「古代海上絲綢之路」的世代繁盛，證明了黃埔古港獨一無二的歷史地位，也反映了廣州滄海桑田的巨大變遷。黃埔村就是一座「古代海上絲綢之路」活的博物館，因為最有價值的歷史就存在於當下人們的內心。

黃埔古港興旺發達時，正是十七世紀到十九世紀廣州海外貿易鼎盛期，也就是近代西方商人津津樂道的「對華貿易的黃金時代」。英國人威廉·希克一七六九年來過廣州，他對廣州讚不絕口：「珠江上船舶運行穿梭的情景，就像倫敦橋下泰晤士河，不同的是，河面的帆船形式不同，還有大帆船，在外國人眼裡再沒有比排列在長達幾里的帆船更為壯觀的了。」

有人這樣評價，處於東方海岸之邊的廣州黃埔古港，一艘艘大船從這裡啟程，揚帆遠航，將絲綢、瓷器、茶葉帶往世界各地的同時，也帶去了農耕及手工業技術、造紙術和指南針，搭乘商船來來往往的高僧、科學家、畫師、譯者更是文化交融的使者。從這個意義上說，在持續千年的歷史長河中，作為海上絲綢之路發祥地之一的廣州，是中華文明影響世界之旅的一大啟程地。

歷史已經遠去，昔日的輝煌逐漸消失在慢慢淤積的古港渡口，碼頭也看不到昔日的忙碌和繁華。歷史需要記憶的承載，建設一個黃埔古港歷史陳列館是個不錯的主意，廣州人也這樣做了。

黃埔古港歷史陳列館利用村內的一個祠堂改造而成，二千平米的面積由「古港遺韻」壁畫區、「扶胥生輝」實物區以及中心展區三部分組成。其中，實物區是陳列館最有特色的部分。設計人員將四散在黃埔古村內的四十多件歷代建築材料，如石梁、石柱、石刻等集中在一起，在院落中營造出一個「殘垣斷壁」的景區。他們沒有選擇把這些文物圍起來展出，是希望讓遊客能夠近距離地感受古港文化的輝煌。

在展館的壁畫區內，橫亙著一幅長三十一米、高一點五米的大型漢白玉描金壁畫。畫內描繪了黃埔古港「一港通商」時期萬船來埠的繁榮景象，「歌德堡號」「中國皇后號」都位列其中。這幅壁畫應該是在一些外國人寫生留下的圖畫的基礎上設計而成。

　　黃埔古港作為中國重要的對外港口，船舶雲集，經濟繁榮，村民也較早接觸外國人及外來文化，不少人外出留學、經商，名人輩出。有清政府、日本、俄國駐新加坡的三國領事胡璇澤，有留美學生、向美國總統索回多付賠款以建清華大學的梁誠，有為護送孫中山脫險拖延病情不治的馮肇憲，還有鐵路專家胡棟朝、農業專家馮銳、經濟學家梁方仲。

　　黃埔村還有個保護一方免受日本軍侵略謎一般的日本媳婦的故事，頗具傳奇色彩。

　　一九〇〇年，黃埔村村民馮佐屏前往日本求學，認識了一位日本姑娘。二人不久結為夫妻。一九二四年，四十多歲的馮佐屏為侍奉父母，加上思鄉情濃，攜家人從日本歸來，回黃埔村定居。

　　為解妻子的思鄉之苦，馮佐屏興建了一棟日式風格的小洋樓送給妻子，使她能安心居住下來。這就是如今坐落在黃埔村惇慵街八號的「日本樓」。

　　日本發動侵華戰爭後廣州淪陷，一隊日軍來到黃埔村，眼看村民即將遭受屠戮。突然，馮佐屏的妻子出現在日軍面前，亮出了一把寶刀。日軍見刀後放下軍刀，崇敬地向刀拜了拜，然後退出了黃埔村。抗戰期間，日軍從未到黃埔村掃蕩。

　　附近村莊的村民得知日軍不敢進黃埔村，便紛紛躲進黃埔村避難。因此，黃埔村又被稱之為「平安村」。一九四四年，馮佐屏的妻子生病過世，葬於黃埔村內山頂。

　　關於這把刀的來歷，在黃埔村流行三種說法。一據說馮妻是日本天皇一位遠親，這把刀是她的嫁妝；二據說她是日本幕府末年將軍的侄女，寶刀是將軍贈予的；第三種說法是她是當年某位首相的侄女，刀由他相贈。

熟知村史的一位老人家更認同第三種說法。「日本是等級森嚴的國家，如果她是皇族或是幕府將軍的親戚，是不可能下嫁異族或平民的。」不管怎樣，日本媳婦對黃埔村的貢獻是實實在在的。

二千年長盛不衰

「哥德堡號」是在歷經艱辛即將到家時「功虧一簣」，而另外一艘中國人更為熟悉的「南海一號」則是離開中國泉州港不久後就沉於海底。

泉州是中國古代的另一個重要港口，唐朝時為世界四大口岸之一，宋元時期為「東方第一大港」，被馬可‧波羅譽 為「光明之城」。馬可‧波羅可能是為數不多的在中國比在 本國更為知名的意大利人。他在《馬可‧波羅遊記》中描述了他在中國的見聞，激起了歐洲人對東方的熱烈嚮往，對以後新航路的開闢產生了巨大的影響。不過，很多人懷疑他對中國的描繪有時稍顯誇張。

與「哥德堡號」只能供後人想像不同，見證海上絲綢之路歷史的「南海一號」則因整體挖掘而能讓我們睹其真顏。

一九八七年，在廣東南部的陽江海域，發現一個距今八百多年的沉船遺址。這個後來被稱為「南海一號」的傢伙，是迄今為止世界上發現的海上沉船中年代最早、船體最大、保存最完整的遠洋貿易商船。據估算，它的長度達到 30.4 米、寬9.8 米，船身（不算桅杆）高約 4 米，排水量達到六百噸以上，載重近八百噸。事實上，我們並不知道這艘船本來的名字，也許本就沒有名字。

「南海一號」在泉州港口裝貨後，也許是遭遇風暴，也許是船底漏水，或是我們不知道的其他原因，最終沉沒海底。對它的打撈，卻已是發現它整整二十年後，並且創造性地使用「整體打撈」的方案，將沉船、文物與其周圍海水、泥沙按照原狀一次性吊浮起運，遷移到廣東海上絲綢之路博物館內，再進行文物整理。

　　沒人不關心「南海一號」裡到底有什麼寶貝。二〇一六年一月五日，總共出土文物 14000 餘件套、標本 2575 件，其中瓷器 13000 餘件套、金器 151 件套、銀器 124 件套、銅器 170 件，銅錢約 17000 枚以及大量動植物標本、船木等。

　　「南海一號」正處在古代海上絲綢之路的航道上。海上絲綢之路是古代連接東西方海道的交通大動脈，因運送的主要大宗貨物是絲綢，所以被叫做海上絲綢之路。隨著運送貨物的變化，它也曾被叫做「海上陶瓷之路」「海上香料之路」。它從中國東南沿海，經過中南半島和南海諸國，穿過印度洋，進入紅海，抵達東非和歐洲。中宋元時期，中國同世界六十多個國家有著直接的「海上絲路」商貿往來。明代鄭和下西洋的成功，海上絲綢之路發展到極盛時期。

　　儘管繁榮異常，但在相當長的一段時間內，海上絲綢之路只是存在於零星的文獻記載中，人們對它知之甚少。直到二十世紀，在航線沿岸港口陸續發現來自中國的瓷器、絲綢等文物，海上絲綢之路的面目才逐漸清晰起來。「南海一號」能為這段歷史的研究提供可信的模本，復原和填補與之相關的一段歷史空白，甚至展現文獻和陸上考古無法提供的信息。

　　中國境內海上絲綢之路主要有廣州、泉州、寧波三個主港和揚州、福州等其他支線港組成。廣州從三世紀三〇年代起，就是海上絲綢之路的主港。它被稱為世界海上交通史上唯一二千多年長盛不衰的大港。

　　二〇一五年，中國正式提出「一帶一路」（The Belt and Road,

縮寫 B&R）倡議，這是「絲綢之路經濟帶」和「二十一世紀海上絲綢之路」的簡稱。它將充分依靠中國與有關國家既有的雙多邊機制，藉助既有的、行之有效的區域合作平台，借用古代絲綢之路的歷史符號，高舉和平發展的旗幟，積極發展與沿線國家的經濟合作夥伴關係，共同打造政治互信、經濟融合、文化包容的利益共同體、命運共同體和責任共同體。

廣州的「伸展」運動

十九世紀時，中美貿易幾乎都在商行之間進行交易。一個名叫伍秉鑑的商人，他的商行在美國久負盛名，生意幾近壟斷。不過，比起他的真名，商名浩官（Howqua）更為美國商 人所熟知，Hu-Kwa Tea 也是因此得名。

二〇一四年，康涅狄格大學副教授、福布斯博物館董事羅伯特・福布斯，在祖輩留下的位於波士頓米爾頓區（Milton） 的祖屋，辦了美國第一家中美貿易博物館（Forbes House Museum）。這家博物館，面積不大，但完好地保存了祖輩從廣州帶回來的每一件物品。

羅伯特・福布斯的高曾祖父也叫羅伯特・福布斯 （Robert Forbes），十三歲時他乘坐一艘商船漂洋過海歷經艱辛來到廣州，投奔開商行的舅舅學做生意。他和伍秉鑑交往密切。離開廣州時，伍秉鑑贈送一幅自畫像以為留念。羅伯特，福布斯就是聽著這些往事，看著精心保存的中國畫像、瓷器慢慢長大的。

伍秉鑑的父親伍國瑩從事對外貿易，並在一七八三年成立了怡和行。伍秉鑑生於一七六九年，三十二歲接手怡和行後，伍家事業快速崛起。大約在他六十歲時，他和他的家族擁有的財產高達二千六百萬銀元。他們不但在國內擁有地產、房產、茶山、店鋪和巨款，而且在美國投資鐵路、證券交易和保險業務，怡和行成為名副其實的跨國財團。

二〇〇一年，《華爾街日報》專門統計了一千年來世界上最富有的五十個人。其中六個入選的中國人是成吉思汗、忽必烈、劉瑾、和珅、伍秉鑑和宋子文。《華爾街日報》評價說：「出生於一七六九年的清朝行商伍秉鑑繼承父業與外商從事買賣，又進一步貸款給外商並以此獲得巨額財富。他在西方商界享有相當高的知名度。」

伍秉鑑被西方商人認為「誠實、親切、細心、慷慨，而且富有」，英國人稱讚他「善於理財，聰明過人」。據說，伍秉鑑經營理念超前，與歐美各國重要客戶建立了緊密聯繫。流傳很廣的一個故事是，一個美國商人因經營不善，欠了伍秉鑑七萬多美元的債務無力償還。伍秉鑑得知後，把借據撕碎，宣布賬目結清，使這位商人得以重返家園。伍秉鑑應該深諳「商標」的重要性，他將自己的肖像附送在銷往海外的茶葉中。儘管這個樣貌清瘦的生意人一生沒離開過廣州，但他的肖像卻隨著貨物走到美洲、英國以及印度。

這位晚清的大生意人，一度是廣州十三行的首富，怡和行也成為廣州十三行發展的縮影。十三行是官府特許經營對外貿易商行的總稱，並不必然是十三個商行。

廣州「一口通商」後，十三行的商人在八十多年的時間裡，成為大清帝國對外的唯一管家。除了做生意之外，來華洋商從貨物買賣到日常起居，事無鉅細，都必須通過十三行才能辦理。

不過，《南京條約》規定開放廣州、廈門、福州、寧波、上海五處為通商口岸（史稱「五口通商」）。十三行不再擁有獨攬中國對外貿易的特權，也就日趨沒落。

十三行曾是廣州的商業中心。它所在的附近區域，包括北京路區域在內，一直是近代以前廣州城的行政中心，廣府文化的中心，也是歷史上最繁華的商業集散地。

　　直到改革開放後，以北京路商圈為核心的老城區中心商業軸和以天河城商圈為核心的新城市中軸線商務發展軸，成為廣州城市和經濟發展雙動力。

　　廣州的變化如此之快。曾經「不到南方大廈，不算到了廣州」的城市地標，到後來的北京路步行街、天河路商圈，再到如今的珠江新城，城市中心的變遷，見證著廣州城市的發展。二〇〇四年，廣州天河區成為新城市中心區。

　　二〇一〇年，廣州亞運會開幕式在珠江上一個名叫海心沙的小島上舉行，海心沙就在這所城市的新中軸線上。有人說，這裡集中了太多的廣州之最——最高的摩天大樓、最大的市民廣場、最大的地下空間、最好的文化建築以及最繁華的中央商務區。

廣交會的開放基因

廣州的「伸展」運動，不僅在於城市的擴張，更在於以開放的心態面向世界，這是深藏在這個城市骨髓裡的基因，也是這個城市獨特的精神氣質。這集中地體現在廣交會上。

一九五七年，中國出口商品交易會在廣州誕生，這個更被人習慣地稱為廣交會的展會，開闢了一條中國與世界交往的通道，它是歷史最長、層次最高、規模最大、商品種類最齊全、到會境外採購商最多、成交效果最好的「中國第一展」。

為什麼要把第一個全國出口商品的展覽會放在廣州舉辦？自有其不為外人所知的原因。廣州作為千年商都，商業氛圍濃厚，地域優勢獨特，是香港、澳門地區以及東南亞商人到中國內地做生意的唯一通道。

二十世紀七〇年代初，廣交會在流花路的新展館啟用。流花展館與廣州火車站近在咫尺，五六公里車程之外就是白雲機場（不過現在它已搬到離市中心更遠的郊區，為示區別，被叫做新白雲機場）。一九八六年，流花路展館與周圍的東方賓館新樓、流花賓館、廣州市新火車站等現代建築群，被評為羊城新八景之一——「流花玉宇」。

羊在中國的文化裡是馴順的代表，因與「陽」同音，有吉祥之意。廣州因與羊有關的一個傳說，又被稱為「羊城」。從宋代開始，這個城市的人們就不斷評選城市的八種名勝景點，稱作「羊城八景」。

二〇〇一年四月，在距離流花展館十多公里的東部琶洲，開始建設新的會展中心，並在二〇〇三年使用。二〇〇八年十月，第一百零四屆廣交會就已全部在琶洲展館舉行。

琶洲，這個黃埔古港所在的地方，利用琶洲會展中心，再次成為廣州向世界敞開交流之門的象徵。

互聯網時代的到來，廣交會也在不斷推陳出新，它搭建電商平台，打造全年三百六十五天不落幕的網上廣交會。廣交會擁抱互聯網，琶洲也熱烈擁抱互聯網，琶洲島西側的互聯網創新集聚區，聚集了騰訊、阿里巴巴、小米、唯品會等幾十家企業，設立總部或項目公司。

其中就包括微信。微信所在的公司名叫騰訊。在微信以前，他們的社交軟件 QQ 一度是最受歡迎的。也許這是一種展示企業雄心的方式，騰訊以十七點六億元獲得琶洲的一塊地以建設微信總部大樓。

相信即便在多年以後，中國人也會記得在這個時代有一款名叫微信的社交軟件，深刻影響著中國人的日常生活。它以「連接一切」作為口號，成為這個時代絕大多數中國人智能手機裡必會安裝的一款軟件。在相當長的一段時間裡，它讓很多中國人的錢包裡不用裝現金，因為在線支付已是如此普及，你在中國偏僻農村的一個小商店裡，也可以通過掃一個名叫二維碼的東西直接付款。整個交易過程，無需使用現金。

二〇一六年第二季度，微信已經覆蓋中國百分之九十四以上的智能手機，月活躍用戶達到八點零六億，用戶覆蓋二百多個國家、超過二十種語言。

微信就誕生在廣州。它用一種特別的方式讓中國與世界連接，讓世界變得更為開放。微信和 QQ 所在只是騰訊公司最具代表性的產品。這家公司的實際負責人馬化騰，最初創業時率領自己的團隊做網頁、做系統集成、做程序設計。但由於不懂市場和市場運作，產品拿出去向運營商推銷，卻經常被拒之門外。這種經歷，相信不管是比爾蓋茨還是喬布斯，應該都曾體會過。

　　二〇一六年十月，中國移動互聯網用戶總數已經達到十點七七億，使用手機上網的用戶數再創歷史新高，總數達到了十點二億，這在全球首屈一指。人們把互聯網的體驗從早前的桌面 PC 帶到了工作生活的方方面面，各個領域都可以永遠在線、實時在線，給所有行業借助微信的力量發展線上線下業務提供了良好基礎，意味著很多的機會。而微信以及與它同類的產品會給中國帶來的改變，還在進行中，遠遠沒有結束。

自貿區：對接世界的「焊點」

以南沙為中心，以五十公里為半徑畫一個圓，可囊括珠三角所有重要城市，包括香港和澳門所有港口碼頭。以一百公里為半徑覆蓋珠三角九座城市和五大國際機場。在地理上，南沙就是珠三角的中心。但它遠遠不是經濟的發展中心。在「發展是硬道理」的中國，南沙卻似乎驗證了中國的一句俗語「燈下黑」——雖處中心卻被有意無意忽略。以致於二十世紀八〇年代，一片荒灘的南沙，被稱為廣州的「西伯利亞」，荒涼而缺少生氣。

但霍英東不這樣看。這是一位香港的實業家，以駁運起家，後從事房地產，他首創了後來通行全國的分期付款模式。二〇〇六年他逝世時，官方通告說他是「中國共產黨的親密朋友」，在中國人的眼中，他是值得信賴的愛國人士。像諸多香港人一樣，霍英東祖籍也在廣東。他曾為家鄉廣州番禺修建洛溪大橋，讓珠江不再是河兩岸交流的交通阻礙。

霍英東在南沙傾注了巨額資金和大量心血。他生前曾多次說過，自己有一個「南沙夢」，希望將南沙建設成廣東乃至全國對外開放的窗口。

一九九二年，霍英東買下南沙濱海地區二十二平方公里土地進行運作開發。二〇〇二年起，先後修建了南沙大酒店、世貿中心大廈等標誌性建築及東發碼頭、南沙客運港、虎門渡輪碼頭、南沙資訊科技園區等。據說，霍英東二十五年在南沙投資六十億。這筆錢可以買下兩個廣州地標建築「小蠻腰」（一個形狀婀娜、400 多米高的電視塔），或者在內地城市打造一個占地近一百萬平方米的旅遊觀光小鎮。

在廣闊的土地上進行開發，僅靠一個企業，速度即使不能說緩慢，但也很難強行說快。

世界上百分之九十的發達城市都在沿海地區。以世界最強大的美國為例，紐約、波士頓、費城、華盛頓、西雅圖、舊金山、洛杉磯、休斯敦、亞特蘭大、邁阿密都是沿海地區。日本全國都是狹長的沿海地區。過去，廣州的發展一直依賴於珠江兩岸，靠水而建，靠水發展。然而，隨著城市的發展，廣州必須從靠水走向靠海，作為廣州唯一靠海的區域，南沙毫無疑問地成為發展的核心。

一切都是好的！南沙和霍家一起，在等待著一個新的契機，現在看來，也許這個契機應該叫「自貿區」。

二〇一四年十二月，國務院決定設立中國（廣東）自由貿易試驗區，廣東自貿區涵蓋三片區：廣州南沙新區片區（廣州南沙自貿區）、深圳前海蛇口片區（深圳前海蛇口自貿區）、珠海橫琴新區片區（珠海橫琴自貿區），總面積一百一十六點二平方公里。

中國自由貿易區是中國深化改革開放的新節點。它是一種多功能經濟性特區，在國境內關外設立，以優惠稅收和海關特殊監管政策為主要手段，以貿易自由化、便利化為主要目的。二〇一三年九月二十九日中國（上海）自由貿易試驗區正式成立，成為中國第一個自貿區。

中國（廣東）自由貿易試驗區其實是分佈在廣州、深圳和珠海三個城市。廣州南沙新區片區的面積達到六十平方公里（含廣州南沙保稅港區 7.06 平方公里）。

在中國（廣東）自由貿易試驗區廣州南沙新區片區的官方網站上，對南沙自貿試驗區有著詳細的介紹：「南沙自貿試驗區致力於構建與國際新規則體系相適應的法治化國際化營商環境，率先實現與港澳服務貿易自由化，打造國際貿易功能集成度高、金融創新服務功能強的國際航運物流中心，形成二十一世紀海上絲綢之路沿線國家和地區科技創新合作的示範基地，建成港澳向內地拓展、內地藉助港澳通達國際市場的雙向通道和重要平台，為國家構建開放型經濟新格局發揮重要作用。」

南沙自貿試驗片區掛牌以來，率先推行「一口受理」新模式，「一照一碼」改革在全國率先拓展至工商、質監、國稅等十三個部門，全國首創政府購買查驗服務、全國首創海關快速驗放機制、全國首創「智檢口岸」……

南沙自貿試驗片區，創造了為人矚目的廣東「自貿區速度」。

深圳：
「後生」城市
緊追世界

小漁村的巨變

　　從一個小漁村發展成一個超級大城市，需要多少年，中國深圳給出的答案是三十年。

　　中國人樂於進行歸類和排序，比如四大發明、武林五大高手，城市也是這樣。二十世紀九〇年代，人們還習慣將最大的三個城市簡稱為「京津滬」（北京、天津和上海）。但在這個世紀開始，這一說法逐步過渡到「北上廣」（北京、上海和廣州），二〇一〇年前後，人們更習慣稱為「北上廣深」，後起之秀深圳在中國的城市格局中已是超級城市，並被廣泛接受。

　　經濟特區的擁躉可說出若干成功典範，最成功的莫過於中國香港附近後來被稱為「深圳奇蹟」的這一個。

　　由於要考慮可能存在的風險，中國不敢一下子在全國范圍實施經濟改革，於是設立了深圳特區來做試驗，有些出乎意料的是，它吸引了成千上萬的外國投資者，在這裡經過檢驗的政策隨即被推廣到其他城市，包括後來的上海。

　　一九八三年，深圳發行中國第一張股票，掀起中國「一夜暴富」的炒股熱潮，土地市場首次拍賣，創造出老闆、下海、股份公司、外來工、炒魷魚、跳槽等新名詞和生活方式……過去三十多年，深圳創下了難以計數的「中國第一」。

　　深圳改革的開始，源於緊鄰海灣的蛇口響起建設號角。袁庚，深圳特區歷史上乃至中國改革開放歷程中最為耀眼的名字之一。他當年在蛇口工業區的銳意改革、種種探索，如今看來，仍然具有時代意義。

招商局，把一八七二年的晚清重臣李鴻章和一九七八年的共產黨員袁庚聯繫在一起。

一八七二年，李鴻章上書同治請求設立招商局，奏摺呈上三天之後被批准。一九七八年十月，袁庚以招商局第二十九代「掌門人」的身分呈報中共中央《關於充分利用香港招商局問題的請示》，請求設立蛇口工業區，也是在三天后獲得認可。

一九七八年，袁庚已是六十一歲，在中國被稱作「過花甲」之年。這個年紀，很多人已安享晚年生活，但袁庚的新事業才剛剛開始。他把「時間就是金錢、效率就是生命」的牌子立在蛇口的大路上，試驗打破幹部終身制，他把指名道姓批評自己的文章一字不差地登報。面對莫須有的指責，袁庚艱難卻也堅定地在蛇口進行改革，從經濟到政治領域，從社會到文化領域。

蛇口的發展變化是深圳改革開放的縮影。

一九七九年至一九八八年袁庚主管特區工作十年間，國務院原副總理谷牧先後十二次到深圳經濟特區檢查。特區初期幾乎所有的重大決策，都是在他的參與下制定實施的。

負責籌辦廣東省三個經濟特區的吳南生最早提出「廣東先走一步」，並以「要殺頭就殺我」的豪言，主動請纓辦特區。

當然，深圳人最感念的人是鄧小平。他為深圳命名「經濟特區」。這發生在一九八四年的一月二十四日至二月五日，鄧小平到廣東時視察深圳。

鄧小平是中國社會主義改革開放和現代化建設的總設計師。在中國，人們更願意尊敬而不失親切地稱他為「小平同志」。

二○○○年十一月，鄧小平雕像在深圳蓮花山頂揭幕，這是中國國內第一座由中央批准、以城市雕塑形式豎立的鄧小平雕像。

蓮花山頂鄧小平銅塑像高六米，重六噸，塑造的小平形象身穿風衣，面朝南方，大步向前，風衣的一角在身後吹起。從蓮花山北面上到山頂，迎面首先看到的是影壁，上面刻著鄧小平的原話：「深圳的發展和經驗證明，我們建立經濟特區的政策是正確的。」繞過影壁另一面能看到用隸書寫的：「我是中國人民的兒子，我深深地愛著我的祖國和人民。」

一九九○年前後，國際國內形勢發生深刻變化，經濟特區和改革開放事業的發展再次面臨阻力。在這樣的關鍵時刻，鄧小平再次來到廣東視察。那是一九九二年一月十九日至一月二十九日，他在深圳視察四天，在珠海視察七天。這一年的一月十八日到二月二十一日，鄧小平先後到武昌、深圳、珠海、上海等地並發表重要談話，提出「要抓緊有利時機，加快改革開放步伐，力爭國民經濟更好地上一個新台階」的要求，為中國走上有中國特色社會主義市場經濟發展道路奠定了思想基礎。

一月二十一日，鄧小平在國貿大廈發表了視察途中最重要的一次講話。「要警惕右，但主要是防『左』。特區發展了十幾年才有今天的樣子，垮起來是一夜之間哪！……只有經濟發展了，人民生活上去了，他們才會相信你，支持你，擁護你。堅持以經濟建設為中心的基本路線不是管十年，二十年，是要管一百年！動搖不得。只要我們不堅持社會主義，不改革開放，不發展經濟，不改善人民生活，走任何一條路，都是死路！」

國貿大廈被稱為「深圳經濟特區的窗口」，也是「中國改革開放的象徵」。

　　一九八四年，高一百六十米、共五十三層的國貿大廈僅十四個月便宣告竣工，創造了「三天一層樓」的奇蹟。主樓開建後，先是七天建一層，後來速度提升到五天、四天一層。從第三十層開始，持續以三天蓋一層的速度。因國貿大廈而開始流傳的「深圳速度」，已經成為一個高速度高效益的新概念，成為改革開放後中國建設發展的象徵。

移民之城

　　三十多年的時間，深圳從一個僅有三萬多人口、兩三條小街的邊陲小鎮，發展成為一座擁有上千萬人口，經濟繁榮、社會和諧、功能完備、環境優美的現代化都市，創造了世界工業化、城市化、現代化史上的奇蹟。

　　在深圳的發展歷程中，更多不知名的人無疑為這個城市的建設也在做著特別的貢獻，這些貢獻看似微不足道，但卻實實在在，並成為推動城市前進的巨大合力。正應了中國的那句古詩「潤物細無聲」，意思是春雨隨著春風在夜裡悄悄地落下，悄然無聲地滋潤著大地萬物。

　　深圳是中國最為典型的移民城市。一九七九年深圳剛剛建市時，下轄人口只有三十幾萬。到二〇一五年底，其常住人口已經達到 1137.89 萬，成為名副其實的移民之城，也是中國最大的移民之城。

　　一九八二年七月，二萬基建工程兵從上海、天津、唐山等地集結南下，集體轉業為建築工人，二十世紀八〇年代深圳四分之一的高樓都出自基建工程兵之手。

　　某種意義上，深圳三十年的歷史就是一部深圳移民的奮鬥史。他們從全國各地攜帶夢想而來，從無到有，和這座城市一起經歷奮鬥、繁榮、迷茫與轉型，一起享受成功，再一起迎接新挑戰。

　　對這些人的褒獎在二〇〇九年達到一個特別的高潮。這一年，美國《時代》週刊評選二〇〇九年年度人物，其中就包括「中國工人」。

「中國工人」作為榜單上的唯一一個群體，排在僅次於美聯儲主席的第二位。《時代》週刊點評說：「中國有這麼一個詞：『保8』，意思是保持每年 8%的經濟增長率，中國政府認為這對確保社會穩定至關重要。儘管一年前許多人認為這是一個夢想，但是中國做到了，在世界主要經濟體中繼續保持最快的發展速度，並帶領世界走向經濟復甦，這些功勞首先要歸功於中國千千萬萬勤勞堅韌的普通工人。」

不管是在歷史還是在當下，中國工人都是一支偉大的、出色的、貢獻卓著的隊伍。新中國成立以來，尤其是改革開放三十多年來，千千萬萬中國工人，用他們辛勤勞動與卓越奉獻，成為推動中國經濟發展和社會全面進步的最重要力量之一。

創新之都

二〇一五年，華為累計申請了五萬二千五百五十件國內專利和三萬零六百一十三件外國專利，專利申請總量位居全球第一。二〇一五年，華為以三千八百九十八件專利申請量蟬聯全球企業專利排名榜首。

不過，申請數量並不意味著一家企業在專利上面的積累和優勢，被授權的專利才可以擁有真正話語權！也就是在二〇一五年，蘋果向華為許可專利九十八件，而華為向蘋果許可專利七百六十九件。

華為手機在中國市場後起直追，直追蘋果和三星，靠的是過硬的品質。

一九八七年註冊成立的華為技術有限公司，是一家生產銷售通信設備的民營通信科技公司，二〇一六年底，他有十七萬多名員工，華為的產品和解決方案已經應用於全球一百七十多個國家，服務全球運營商五十強中的四十五家及全球三分之一的人口。從服務國家和人口來說，華為是一個全球化的公司，但它的總部在深圳。它就是一家在深圳發展起來的公司。

華為成為深圳創新的象徵，也是深圳這個城市創新發展的展示。深圳因創新而生，已成為中國人心目中的「創客之都」「創新之城」。除了華為，深圳還有中興、騰訊、大疆以及華大基因等知名公司。

一九九八年成立的騰訊公司，是中國最大的互聯網綜合服務提供商之一，也是中國服務用戶最多的互聯網企業之一。騰訊最為中國人熟知的產品是 QQ 和微信，在某種程度上，這兩款產品名稱已有著自身的含義，就像中國人提到蘋果不會以為它僅僅只是一種水果，還應是一家美國公司以及它生產的產品。

騰訊公司董事會主席馬化騰十三歲來到深圳，一九九八年帶著五個人的團隊和五十萬元的資金研發出了 QQ 軟件。資金和技術一度成為騰訊發展的瓶頸，讓馬化騰夜不能寐。最困難的時候，他幾度想賣掉QQ。但他堅持下來的結果是，二〇一五年六月，騰訊市值在全球互聯網公司中排名第五，二〇一四年年收入七百八十九億元。

在前沿科技領域創新創業的大疆創新科技有限公司與華大基因同樣被視為深圳創新典範。大疆創新被稱作是無人機界的神級公司，占據全球無人機半數以上的市場份額，它的產品已被用於航拍、電影、農業、新聞、能源、遙感測繪等眾多領域，並不斷地融入新的行業應用。華大基因則通過基因科技造福人類，這家成立於一九九九年的公司，是全球最大的基因組學研發機構。它以「產學研」一體化的創新發展模式引領基因組學的發展，通過遍布全球的分支機構與產業鏈各方建立廣泛的合作，將前沿的多組學科研成果應用於醫學健康、農業育種、資源保存等領域，推動基因科技成果轉化，實現基因科技造福人類。華大基因入選二〇一五年全球成長型公司。一般來說，全球成長型公司被視為市場的開拓者、創新者與塑造者。

如果說深圳僅僅是由這些明星公司來代言城市的創新能力，是不全面的。「自主創新」已成為這座城市發展的主導戰略。深圳全社會研發投入逐年提升，二〇一五年占 GDP 比重已升至 4.05%,相當於全 國平均水平的兩倍。PCT （專利合作條約）國際專利申請量和每萬人 發明專利擁有量居中國各大中城市首位，4G 技術、基因測序、超材 料、3D 顯示等領域創新能力躋身世界前沿。

二〇一四年，深圳 PCT 國際專利申請量達到一點一六萬件，同比增長 15.9%，連續十一年居全國各大中城市之首；每萬人發明專利擁有量 達到六十六點七件，居全國各大中城市首位。在福布斯發布的「中美創新 人物」名單中，中國有十人，深圳占五席。在二〇一四年中國科學十大 進展中，深圳兩項研究成果入選。企業成為深圳的市場主體，成為 創新主體。

作為全球創新鏈上最為獨特的創新之城、中國一線城市中最年輕的城市，深圳一直不斷探尋新的經濟增長動力，發展為最適合全球創客的舞台。

▍山寨遠去，智慧歸來

經過改革開放三十多年的積累，深圳已擁有較為完善的上下游產業鏈，形成了硬件領域科技、資本、信息、人才的聚集。國內最大的開源硬件製造商——矽遞科技創始人潘昊談及來深圳創業的初衷時說，自己在華強北轉了一天，就被這裡完美的硬件配套所折服。國際知名機構、硬件孵化中心 HAXLR8R 的創始人 Cyril Eberssweiler 把總部從硅谷搬到了深圳，他說：「這裡能夠讓我們在一公里之內找到任何想要的原材料，這是美國、歐洲和世界上任何地方都做不到的，因為那裡沒有深圳的華強北。」另一名落戶深圳的印度創客也表示，不管多複雜的設計，在這裡不到一週的時間就能生產出樣品來。

在深圳，華強北周邊不超過一公里的範圍內，就能找到創客想要的所有原材料，不到一週的時間，就能完成「產品原型—產品—小批量生產」的整個過程，而成本可能只相當於硅谷的 1% 到 5%。一名中關村早期創業者問兒子：「為什麼一定要大老遠跑到深圳辦公司？」兒子回答說，找一塊 IC，在深圳兩個星期就夠了，但在別的地方可能要兩個月；做一塊 PCB 板，深圳及周邊地區加工廠多，質量好又便宜。這就是深圳的製造業基礎加上市場經濟高度發育積累起來的產業鏈優勢。這種優勢讓創新在深圳變成更便捷，讓深圳變成了「創客天堂」。

華強北，日均人流量曾達到約五十萬人次，年交易額超三千億元，是全國規模最大、科技含量最高、產品種類最齊全、年交易額最大的電子產品交易集散地，一度被視為中國電子行業的「風向標」和「晴雨表」。這裡的電子元器件交易量占深圳市電子通訊市場總數的 95%。

不過，巨大的交易下，各種仿造的電子產品也不斷出現。一款蘋果手機上市，一個月後也許在華強北花幾百塊錢就能買到一個外形極其相似的手機，只是商標從蘋果換成被咬了一口的橘子。它們用低廉的價格與極快的出新速度，將那些既需要內部檢測又需要入網檢測的國產手機品牌打得落花流水。

也正因此，華強北一度被視為「山寨」的代名詞，被最大的「山寨」手機生產地之名所累。

「山寨」本義指山中的城寨，更多的是被指為模仿、複製、抄襲而來的產品。

如果說山寨手機還能賺取利潤，在山寨平板電腦時代，兩百塊左右的平板電腦到處都是。山寨廠家們用白菜價迅速在深圳紮根成長，再被白菜價逼得關門歇業，退出市場。

山寨和創新其實是硬幣的兩面。「當大多人忽視了類似華強北中小企業的時候，更多人覺得這些企業只會山寨，我們相信他們是產業變革的力量。」阿里巴巴技術委員會主席王堅在《在線》一書中這樣認為。

Fab Lab 創始人尼爾・哥申菲爾德就認為山寨也是非常好的創新方式。他說，自己喜歡華強北，給兒子買了一個像 AppleWatch 的產品，比 AppleWatch 更好，裡面還有手機功能。做這種手錶，要有這 樣那樣的功能，這也是先進性的技術。在 Fab2.0 里，我們也可以做一些個性化製造，對所有的功能進行設計、建模、分裝等，去研究怎樣複製這個功能，而不是做一個假的 AppleWatch。」「我們所說的 複製，是指你有能力超越產品現在的功能範圍。」

二〇一〇年底，深圳開始組織打擊侵犯知識產權和制售假冒偽劣商品的專項行動，持續了半年以上，最終導致三千六百餘商戶退出華強北電子市場，進行了一次大規模的手機行業洗牌。

此外，由於深圳地鐵七號線施工，自二〇一三年三月起，華強北主幹道進行了圍擋，改造提升，華強北一度出現空鋪現象嚴重、租金持續下滑的現象。

二〇一六年底，華強北重新開街，並首次以「步行街」身分嶄新亮相。過去三十年，華強北成長為「中國電子第一街」。未來五到十年，華強北將致力於成為「全國最具影響力、輻射海內外的高端電子信息服務、展示和交易中心、多元業態混合的高品質商業中心和生產型服務業中心，兼有商務辦公、居住等功能的城市綜合性片區」。

深圳對創新有著清晰的認識，要建立一個綜合創新生態體系，通過創新鏈把各種創新要素形成一個正向的振盪，就是科研資金最早投入，最後通過成果，通過金融創新走下來，走到最後再回到科研創新進行新一輪的更高技術、更高水平的創新，形成一個正向的振盪。

佛山：佛光普照的城市

把中國菜「炒」到全世界

順德，與東莞、中山、南海並稱「廣東四小虎」，「二〇一四中國百強區第一名」。在中國的基本話語體系中，進入排行榜單的前列，說明這個城市的與眾不同。

順德意為「順天明德」，這是廣東佛山市的一個區，它自古經濟發達，商業繁榮，文教鼎盛。

二〇一四年十二月，聯合國教科文組織向順德頒發了「世界美食之都」牌匾，順德正式成為聯合國教科文組織全球創意城市網絡組織的成員。

當時，全球有六座城市被聯合國教科文組織授予的「美食之都」，分別是哥倫比亞的波帕揚、中國成都、瑞典的厄‧特松德、黎巴嫩扎赫勒、韓國全州、中國佛山的順德。

聯合國教科文組織駐京辦主任辛格說：「順德作為粵菜中的代表，有非常優越的特色，而且在世界各地都有順德的餐館，這個是順德美食能推向全世界的一個很重要的地方。今後，我們也將會提供一個更國際化的平台協助順德美食推廣到全世界。」

美食，成為順德——這個面積不到一千平方公里的城市——最重要的標籤之一。中國人對美食文化情有獨鍾，所以古代的諺語即有「民以食為天」。

粵菜即廣東菜，是中國傳統四大菜系之一。狹義上的粵菜指廣州府菜，包括順（德）、南（海）、番（禺）。

粵菜因其選料嚴格、做工精細、中西結合、質鮮味美、養生保健等特點而名揚天下。作為在海外影響力最大的中國菜系，粵菜館遍布全球，因此有「有華人的地方就有粵菜」的說法。

順德是粵菜最重要的發源地之一，它是佛山的五個區之一，順德的美食文化也是佛山的縮影。據不完全統計，佛山市登記在冊的廚點師就有近千人，其中很多是國家級特級烹飪大師。

二〇一四年的統計數據顯示，順德有「中國烹飪大師」九位、「中國烹飪名師」三十四位、「中華餐飲名店」二十一家、「中華名小吃」十一種，是國內烹飪大師、餐飲名店最密集的地區之一。二〇〇四年，被中國烹飪協會評為「中國廚師之鄉」；二〇一〇年又獲評「中華美食名城」。順德平均每十七個人當中就有一個人從事餐飲行業。

一個世紀以來，佛山餐飲業群星閃耀，湧現了眾多的著名廚師。上世紀二〇至三〇年代，譚傑南在廣州開辦的陶陶居、七妙齋和大同酒家，至今仍享有盛名。

「陶陶居」寓意來此品茗樂也陶陶。陶陶居是廣州最有名氣的茶樓之一，主要經營名茶、茶點、茶食及酒菜餐飲。廣東人喜歡飲茶，尤其喜歡去茶館喝早茶，茶客坐定，服務員前來請茶客點茶和糕點，早茶也成為廣州的獨特城市文化。

上世紀三〇至五〇年代佛山名廚有崔強、黎和、王瑞、陸貞，被譽為廣東飲食業的四大天王；五〇至六〇年代有羅坤、潘同。尤為難得的是，順德兩位國廚蕭良初、康輝為主廚的團隊，先後開創了上海、北京之南北國宴。蕭良初從一九五一年作為首任總廚任職新中國第一個國賓館——上海錦江飯店，先後為一百多個國家的國王、總統、首相、總理等政要主廚或安排菜式。

一九五四年周恩來總理參加日內瓦會議，蕭良初是隨行廚師。其間周總理請喜劇大師卓別林吃飯，主賓談興甚歡，卓別林吃完意猶未盡，專門請蕭良初加做了一道香酥雞，打包回家與家人分享。

　　一九六一年，周恩來總理率領中國代表團出席日內瓦擴大會議。蕭良初被點名隨團掌勺，其拿手菜八珍鹽焗雞等佳餚得到各國貴賓贊賞。

　　康輝曾任北京飯店行政總廚，併負責籌建釣魚台國賓館和人民大會堂餐廳。二○○二年，他成為被授予國寶級的中國十二位「中國烹飪大師」之一。

中國功夫「漂洋」去

一九九九年《時代週刊》列出二十世紀英雄與偶像人物名單，在這份榜單中，有英國已故黛安娜王妃、拳王阿里、瑪麗蓮，夢露、美國總統肯尼迪、球王貝利。但對中國人來說，最為熟悉的應該是這位黃皮膚、拍照時經常一臉桀驁不馴的功夫巨星李小龍，他就是中國功夫的代言人，就像邁克爾‧喬丹是籃球的標誌、貝利是現代足球的標誌。

二〇〇〇年，美國政府宣布發行一套《李小龍誕辰六十週年紀念郵票》，這是繼瑪麗蓮‧夢露和 007 後第三位獲此殊榮的藝人，也是華人第一人。二〇〇三年美國《黑帶》雜誌推出李小龍逝世三十週年紀念專輯，表明「李小龍對美國武術界的恆久影響」。

Kung fu，英語中這樣稱呼中國功夫，這本是佛山和珠江三角洲中部地區對武術的俗稱。在語言翻譯中，直接音譯或者是因為它難以翻譯，或者是因為它很重要，功夫顯然應屬後者。讓世界迷上中國功夫的人無疑就是李小龍。

李小龍的祖籍就在廣東順德均安鎮，順德所在的佛山市，是中國的功夫之鄉。全球最大的李小龍紀念館就在均安鎮，這個總用地面積達到三點七萬平方米的大型展館在二〇〇八年開始對外開放。

佛山是中國南派功夫的主要發源地。二〇〇四年，佛山被授予中國「武術之城」稱號。明初，佛山功夫已相當普及。清末民初，佛山功夫流派紛呈，湧現出一批有國際影響的武術名家和武術組織，並通過各種途徑走向世界，世界上廣泛流行的蔡李佛拳、洪拳、詠春拳等不少拳種和流派其根都在佛山，著名武術大師黃飛鴻、詠春宗師梁贊、葉問祖籍及師承亦在佛山。

李小龍為太多人所熟知。他是世界武道變革先驅者、武術技擊家、武術哲學家、UFC 開創者、MMA 之父、武術宗師、功夫片的開創者和截拳道創始人、華人武打電影演員、中國功夫首位全球推廣者、好萊塢首位華人演員。他在香港的四部半電影三次打破多項紀錄，其中《猛龍過江》打破了亞洲電影票房紀錄，與好萊塢合作的《龍爭虎鬥》全球總票房達二點三億美元。美國報刊甚至把李小龍譽為「功夫之王」，日本人稱他為「武之聖者」，香港報紙也讚譽他為「當代中國武術及電影史上的奇才」。

正是在李小龍之後，中國多位功夫明星走上世界舞台。其中就包括成龍和李連杰。

與李小龍直接展示功夫的剛硬不同，成龍將武術與戲曲雜耍嫁接，在注重動作的觀賞性同時，減少了功夫電影中常見的血腥暴力場面，開創了功夫喜劇的先河。

回首當年，李小龍出生在美國，但他的童年和少年時光是在香港度過。小時候的李小龍身體十分瘦弱，父親為了強壯兒子的體魄，便教其打太極拳。李小龍自己本就喜歡嘗試新事物，酷愛冒險，特別是戶外運動。於是他迷上了武術，除了太極拳，他還學過詠春拳、洪拳、少林拳等拳種，為今後自創打下了基礎。

一九六七年，李小龍在美國創立了跨越門派限制的、世界性的現代中國功夫「科學的街頭格鬥技」——截拳道（Jeet Kune Do），那年他二十七歲。這是一種融合世界各種武術精華的全方位自由搏擊術。但很多人認為，截拳道中有詠春拳的影子。毫無疑問，這來自於他的師傅葉問。

一八九三年出生的葉問，祖籍廣東省南海縣桑園，上世紀五〇年代開始在香港教授詠春拳。其封門弟子梁挺將詠春拳傳揚國際，更通過其子弟在全球廣泛傳揚，形成出一套最權威的中國傳統武術實戰修習課程《梁挺詠春》（WingTsun），載譽全球。葉問一九七二年去世後，其子葉准、葉正致力於向海外推廣詠春拳術，葉准還曾獲得美國奧委會的嘉獎。

另外一位中國功夫明星李連杰生於北京，他創紀錄地在一九七五年至一九七九年間連續五年獲得中國武術全能冠軍。如果不是在一九八二年主演電影《少林寺》，他可能只是一個優秀的武術隊員而不是武打明星。

《少林寺》引起的轟動，可以用下面的事實說明：這部內地以當時一角錢的票價，累計票房達一億元人民幣。也就是說，他的電影曾被至少觀看十億次。

李連杰拍攝的最為經典的電影就是《黃飛鴻》系列。九〇年初，李連杰接受邀請出演《黃飛鴻之壯志凌雲》，在香港引起轟動，之後他一連拍了五部《黃飛鴻》系列電影。在中國，以黃飛鴻為主題拍攝的電影多達上百部，創造世界之最。

當然，電影中的黃飛鴻並非與現實完全相符。黃飛鴻一八五六年出生於佛山市南海縣，他是清末民初的洪拳大師，嶺南武術界一代宗師。在南派武術的發展中有著重要的影響，他的一生充滿傳奇色彩，曾追隨著名愛國將領劉永福在抗日保台戰爭中立下功勛。他還是位濟世為懷、救死扶傷名醫。他還善於舞獅，有廣州獅王之稱。

佛山夢想

　　美食和功夫讓佛山譽滿天下，成為文化名城和廣府文化的核心地帶。但被譽為全國先進製造業基地、廣東重要的製造業中心，對佛山來說，也同樣重要。

　　佛山「肇跡於晉，得名於唐」。五百年前，中國正值明朝中後期，在這個傳統農業大國之內，生產分工更加細化，出現了脫離農業耕作的手工業階層。那時的中國，出現了商品經濟的萌芽，有四個地方尤為突出，被稱為「中國四大名鎮」。它們是：湖北漢口鎮，江西景德鎮，河南朱仙鎮，以及我們熟悉的廣東佛山鎮。

　　我們要講述的城市──佛山，這個五百年前登上中國歷史舞台的名鎮，正是利用這一時期，迅速崛起成為華南的經濟、商貿和文化中心。

　　明清時期，佛山逐步發展成嶺南地區商品集散地和冶鑄、陶瓷、紡織、中成藥等四大製造業中心。

　　石灣位於佛山禪城區東南部，這裡的陶瓷早就成為佛山亮麗的「名片」，「石灣瓦，甲天下，旁及海外之國」。明、清兩代，方圓幾公里的石灣小鎮就有陶瓷一百零七座，從業人數達六萬多人。因為石灣陶瓷，佛山才有了「南國陶都」的聲譽。「都」在中國的話語體系中，有一個含義是「頭目，首領」，意思是最好的。改革開放後，石灣陶瓷範圍更廣，品種更多樣，規模也更龐大。

　　更為不可思議的是，佛山不是藥材產地，不是棉花產地，沒有鐵礦，也沒有陶泥，但卻成就了四大製造業中心。有人形象地稱其為「無中生有」。事實上，佛山手工業的興盛，與外來人口的南遷離不開關係。南宋後期，中原人口為避戰事南遷，手工業者隨之南遷。到明清時期，佛山手工業發展到達巔峰，遍布全鎮有六百二十多條大小街巷，六十多處渡口，鎮內形成了專業街市有二十八鋪，各行各業興旺發達。

一八七二年，三十六歲的廣東南海西樵簡村人陳啟沅從南洋返回家鄉。第二年，他用自己設計的機器，創辦了我國一家民族資本繅絲業企業。二十五歲時，他就隨兄長到越南經商致富，或許是為了對「繼續昌盛興隆」的美好期待，廠子取名「繼昌隆」。

繼昌隆繅絲廠規模很大，由於經營得法，生意暢旺，產品遠銷海內外，收益頗豐。為了榮耀鄉梓，他大興土林，在簡村建造了當時極具豪華的「百業坊」住宅群，成為名揚天下的大富商。

繼昌隆繅絲廠是中國第一家民族資本經營的機器繅絲廠，它的成立標誌著繅絲工業進入了新的歷史時期，促進了珠江三角洲乃至全國繅絲工業的發展。

佛山還誕生了中國第一家火柴廠——巧明火柴廠，那是清光緒五年（1879 年），創始人衛省軒青年時目睹火柴從國外輸入，令財源外流。於是，他到日本學習火柴生產技術，回國後在佛山文昌沙創辦巧明火柴廠。

以中國第一家新式繅絲廠和第一家火柴廠作為標誌，引領風氣之先的佛山成為中國近代民族工業的發源地之一。

如今，佛山成為珠三角經濟區重要的商貿中心之一，全國流通領域物流示範城市，擁有一批投資規模大、輻射能力強的物流交易配送中心。佛山是中國六個品牌之都之一、國家商標戰略實施示範城市、中國品牌經濟城市。以製造業發達著稱的佛山市，工業發展歷史源遠流長，尤其是傳統製造業優勢明顯，擁有包括「美的」「海天」等一批具有較好工業旅遊要素的知名企業。以石灣陶藝為代表的陶瓷製造業，集聚了上百家各類工業用瓷磚及衛浴產品；以香云紗、綵燈、玉器等為代表的歷史悠久藝術產業，成為人文歷史類的完美代表；以海天醬油、順德製糖為代表的食品工業，見證了嶺南食品產業的歷史發展過程。

東莞：製造業
名城艱難爬坡

兩城之間的奇蹟

　　東莞，位於珠江口東岸。珠江，中國第三大河，在廣東流入大海，包括東莞在內的多個城市受其滋養，被稱為珠江三角洲，這是中國經濟最發達的地區之一。特別是，東莞是在廣州、深圳兩個大城市的中間，距離廣州和深圳中心城區均不到一小時的車程，卻奇蹟般地創造了完全不同於這兩者的生長之路，保持著自己的精神特色。

　　曾有外國專家說「十多年前從衛星地圖上看，廣州和深圳之間還是一片空白，幾年間在這片空白處冒出了一座城市。」不得不說，這是中國城建史和經濟史上的奇蹟。

　　東莞是中國城市乃至中國發展的縮影，快得讓人目瞪口呆。莞城是東莞的一個鎮，鎮在中國是縣和縣級市以下的行政區劃單位。通常地級市下設縣，縣下設鎮。但東莞成為「特殊的一個」，是中國為數不多的不設區、縣的地級市，被俗稱為「直筒子」市。

　　莞城只是東莞三十多個街道和鎮中的一個，但它一直以來都是東莞市的政治、經濟和文化中心，具有悠久的歷史和深厚的文化底蘊。

　　在中國，文化底蘊主要體現在一個城市的歷史中。廣東清代四大名園之一、全國重點文物保護單位可園坐落在這座千年古城。可園的意思就是這個庭園「可堪游賞」。可園又是當時文人雅集地。作為全國重點文物單位，可園在近代廣東藝術史和建築史上都占有重要地位。

中國人習慣講唐詩宋詞，蘇軾在文、詩、詞三方面都達到了極高的造詣，堪稱宋代文學最高成就的代表。他與東莞的資福寺就有不為人知的淵源，他不僅曾夜宿資福寺，還於西元一一〇〇年寫下三篇文章，名為《廣州東莞縣資福禪寺羅漢閣記》《廣州東莞縣資福寺舍利塔銘》《廣州東莞資福堂老柏再生贊》，流傳至今。

在百度搜索中輸入「莞城」二字，最先呈現的搜索結果裡有名為「文化莞城」的網頁，可見文化在莞城中的獨特地位以及給這座城市留下的痕跡，其實這是莞城街道辦的官方網站。百度可以簡單理解成中國的 google，在中文的網絡搜索世界裡最為知名，它的名字據說來源於中國知名的一句詩詞：眾裡尋他千百度，驀然回首，那人卻在燈火闌珊處。這是宋朝時又一位著名的詞人辛棄疾的代表作品，這句話的意思是「我在人群中尋找她千百回，猛然一回頭，不經意間卻在燈火零落之處發現了她」。尋她千百回，正是網絡搜索的真實寫照。

網站對莞城做了這樣的介紹：東莞市莞城街道有一千七百多年的悠久歷史，從唐至德二年（757 年）以來，一直是東莞（縣）市治的所在地。文化源遠流長，文物古蹟眾多。

不僅是「虎門銷煙」

東莞被中國人熟知更多是因為「虎門銷煙」。十九世紀八〇年代，由於鴉片輸入的急遽增加，使中英兩國的貿易地位完全改變。英國由原來的入超變為出超，中國卻相反，造成白銀大量外流。據統計，一八二〇至一八四〇年間，中國外流白銀在一億兩左右。由鴉片大量輸入而引起的白銀不斷外流，已開始擾亂清王朝的國庫和貨幣的流通，使清朝的經濟面臨崩潰的邊緣。更為嚴重的是，鴉片的氾濫極大地摧殘了吸食者的身心健康，任何一個國家都不可能任其發展。一八三九年六月，中國的清朝政府委任欽差大臣林則徐在廣東虎門集中銷毀鴉片。從六月三日到二十五日，二十三天的時間銷毀鴉片一萬九千一百八十七箱和二千一百一十九袋，總重量一百多萬公斤。虎門，這個東莞臨海的小鎮，因揭開了中國近代史的這一頁，聞名中外。

林則徐一生力抗外敵入侵，因其主張嚴禁鴉片，在中國有「民族英雄」之譽。但他對於西方的文化、科技和貿易則持開放態度，主張學其優而用之。根據文獻記載，他至少略通英、葡兩種外語，且著力翻譯西方報刊和書籍。晚清思想家魏源將林則徐及幕僚翻譯的文書合編為《海國圖志》，此書對晚清的洋務運動乃至日本的明治維新都有啟發作用。

「虎門銷煙」讓虎門這個東莞小鎮成為中國人心目中儘管沒去過但一定聽過的地方。不過，一個城市獲得尊重不可能僅靠歷史上的那些瞬間。東莞在改革開放以來創造出的「東莞奇蹟」，被譽為

「中國改革開放一個精彩而生動的縮影」，成為中國改革開放的先進典型，才是我們對這個城市不斷投射關注更重要的原因。

中國共產黨第十一屆中央委員會第三次全體會議召開。諾貝爾經濟學獎得主、新制度經濟學鼻祖羅納德·哈里·科斯在關於中國市場經濟之路的著作《變革中國》中這樣評價這次會議：「是共和國歷史上意義重大的一次會議，它不僅重新鞏固了中國共產黨的政權，還為重新凝聚千瘡百孔的社會鋪平了道路。會議將中國人民的能量、熱忱和創造力重新拉回到社會主義現代化建設上。」

在這前後，中國逐步明確實行對內改革、對外開放的政策。

一九七八年十一月，安徽省鳳陽縣小崗村開始實行「分田到戶，自負盈虧」的家庭聯產承包責任制，拉開了中國對內改革的大幕。一九七九年七月，廣東、福建兩省被正式批准在對外經濟活動中實行特殊政策、靈活措施，邁開了改革開放的歷史性步伐。

改革開放前，東莞一個完全勞動力的日收入最低只有幾分錢。但三十年後的二〇〇八年，東莞經濟年平均增長百分之十八，創造了比亞洲「四小龍」起飛時速度更快、週期更長的高增長奇蹟，成為中國經濟發展最快的地區之一，綜合經濟實力位居全國大中城市第十二位。而事實上，東莞的面積與內地不少縣城相比，並不大多少甚至更小。

「亞洲四小龍」在英文世界被稱為「Four Asian Tigers」（亞洲四虎）。龍是中華民族最具代表性的文化象徵之一。亞洲四小龍指的是從二十世紀六〇年代開始，中國香港、新加坡、韓國和中國台灣推行 出口導向型戰略，重點發展勞動密集型的加工產業，在短時間內實現了經濟的騰飛，一躍成為全亞洲發達富裕的地區，曾被認為是亞洲經濟崛起的代表。在相當長的時間內，「亞洲四小龍」成為中國尤其是沿海省份的楷模。

一九九二年，鄧小平視察南方時曾提出，廣東應爭取在二十年裡趕超「亞洲四小龍」。廣東是東莞所在的省份，它的經濟總量曾長期是中國經濟總量的七分之一。如果對標世界上的國家經濟，廣東與韓國相當，排名世界十幾位。

通過廣東的發展可以看出東莞發展的脈絡。世界銀行前首席亞太經濟學家卡拉斯曾對「東莞奇蹟」驚嘆不已：「東莞，中國南方的一個城市，它在過去二十年一直保持著每年百分之二十的增長速度，在它境內可獲得百分之九十五製造和組裝電腦所需的零部件，它被譽為『世界工廠』。

卡拉斯還在他的學術報告《東亞復興：增長的理念》中談到，東莞在一九七八年時只是珠江邊一片大大小小的村鎮，其人口主要靠捕魚和耕田為生，但在今天東莞有接近七百萬的人口，五百多萬是外來員工，散布在數以千計的工廠，創造出一系列令人眼花繚亂的產品。

東莞模式

東莞的祕訣何在？或者說中國經濟快速發展的祕訣何在？答案之一，也可能是最重要的答案：利用外資，走外向型經濟發展道路。

一九七八年七月，國務院（中央人民政府，是中國最高國家權力機關的執行機關，是最高國家行政機關）頒發了《開展對外加工裝配業務試行辦法》，廣東作為中國改革開放的先行地區和前沿陣地，率先作出發展來料加工的決定。東莞利用自己的地緣優勢和華僑港澳同胞眾多的人緣優勢，開始了引進外資。因資金、技術、人才不足，以「三來一補」作為加工貿易的起步。

「三來一補」指的是來料加工、來樣加工、來件裝配和補償貿易，是中國內地在改革開放初期嘗試性地創立的一種企業貿易形式，「三來一補」企業主要的結構是：由外商提供設備（包括由外商投資建廠房）、原材料、來樣，併負責全部產品的外銷，由中國企業提供土地、廠房、勞力。中外雙方組成一個新的「三來一補「企業。

中國內地第一家「三來一補」企業——太平手袋廠就在東莞誕生。這家一九七八年九月十五日成立，工商批文號是粵字 001 號的企業，前身是虎門太平竹器社。

一九七八年七月，有兩三百人的香港信孚手袋製品公司，因不斷上漲的成本被逼到瀕臨倒閉的邊緣。老闆張子彌帶著幾個手袋和一些碎布料，來到東莞虎門，找到了一個叫唐志平的年輕人。

二十六歲的唐志平當時在太平服裝廠負責供銷業務。張子彌拿出一個黑色女裝手袋和一些手袋半成品的裁片，希望太平服裝廠照樣子儘快仿製。

　　曾經有中國的媒體這樣報導當時的情景：（張子彌）從包裡拿出一個黑色的人造革手袋，給在場工人出了一道他們從未做過的題，即在沒有任何圖紙和說明的情況下，複製這個手袋。於是，從未見過這種手袋的太平服裝廠的三個工人，根據香港客人提供的「吝嗇」的毛料，熬了一個通宵，終於用縫紉機按版呈現了一個一模一樣的手袋。客人很滿意，一個月後便與東莞二輕局簽訂了為期五年的合同（太平服裝廠是東莞二輕局下面的一個企業），東莞第一家「三來一補」企業正式揭開了它的面紗。

　　太平手袋廠位於虎門鎮解放路七號，曾經發生「虎門銷煙」的這個地方，又在創造著一個中國的第一。當年風光無限的「粵字001號」，在一九九六年倒閉，但由於它身上無可取代的歷史標籤，被包括東莞人在內的國人屢屢提及。

　　東莞利用外資的星星之火迅速被點燃，「三來一補」企業在東莞像雨後春筍般發展起來。

　　一九八八年底，東莞「三來一補」企業達二千五百多家，遍布百分之八十的鄉村。一九九一年，引入外資高達十七億美元。東莞從一個默默無聞的農業小縣城，一躍成為一個全國知名的工業化城市。

　　「三來一補」企業的成功引起了全國的關注，這種發展方式也被全國各地廣泛採用，吸引外資發展經濟成為全國潮流。沿海地區許多地方派人來考察學習，借鑑東莞的成功做法。一些媒體和經濟學者也駐足東莞，將其總結成享譽全國的「東莞模式」。

「不管黑貓白貓，捉到老鼠就是好貓」，被譽為中國改革開放總設計師的鄧小平的「白貓黑貓」論，表達了想問題辦事情一切要從實際出發，而不是從條條框框出發的觀點；一切要從有利於發展社會生產力，增強國家綜合國力，提高人民生活水平的實際出發，社會主義是靠幹出來的，不是靠講出來的。「白貓黑貓」論無疑倡導了一種實幹精神。同樣廣為流傳的「摸著石頭過河」，也是要強調邊干邊摸索經驗。正是因為這樣，不同的地方根據基本情況做的發展探索就會被總結概括，成為某種模式。

「東莞模式」一度成為我國實施沿海發展戰略的基本模式，它與「蘇南模式」「溫州模式」齊名，各自代表不同類型的經濟發展模式。不無巧合的是，這三種模式恰恰發生在中國經濟實力較強的幾個省份：「蘇南模式」在江蘇省，「溫州模式」的浙江省，「東莞模式」在廣東省。

「蘇南模式」指的是蘇南的蘇州、無錫和常州通過發展鄉鎮企業實現非農化發展的方式。蘇南模式的主要特徵是：農民依靠自己的力量發展鄉鎮企業；鄉鎮企業的所有制結構以集體經濟為主；鄉鎮政府主導鄉鎮企業的發展；市場調節為主要手段。

溫州人被稱為中國的猶太人，是全中國對市場最敏銳的人群之一，他們總能捕捉到許多市場機會，最先發現市場需求。在市場的孕育下，溫州人全力發展輕工製造業。一下子家庭作坊遍布全城，溫州人的小商品迅速聞名世界。以此為基礎的「溫州模式」是指浙江省東南部的溫州地區以家庭工業和專業化市場的方式發展非農產業，從而形成小商品、大市場的發展格局。小商品是指生產規模、技術含量和運輸成本都較低的商品。大市場是指溫州人在全國建立的市場網絡。

新的發展需求甚至對政府的管理服務也提出了新要求。東莞為適應改革開放、招商引資的需要，率先成立了全國第一個加工貿易服務辦公室，對來東莞辦企業的實行一條龍服務，各部門集中在一起解決企業和百姓辦事難的問題，大大加速了外資進入東莞的速度。

二〇〇七年，東莞在只占全國 0.03% 的土地上，創造了占全國 1.3% 的生產總值、1.1% 的財政收入、4.9% 的出口總額，超越了內地一些省份的經濟能量，故外界以「富可敵省」來形容東莞的經濟能力。

就是在經濟發展過程中，似乎是悄無聲息地，東莞迅速進行著城市化進程，從農業縣到工業大市。一九九〇年前後，當時東莞農村到處出現了「村村點火、戶戶冒煙」的繁榮景象。有人將其概括為「城鄉一體化的農村城市化道路」。

二〇一六年中國城鎮化率達到 57.35%。有數據預測，二〇二〇年，中國的城市化率將達到 60%。而在一九七八年，這一數字僅僅是 17.9%。城市化是人類進步必然要經過的過程，經過了城市化，標誌著現代化目標的實現。

一九八四年，全國農村的改革和發展還處於完善家庭聯產承包責任制的階段，東莞已經完成了農村經濟管理體制，開始向商品農業轉變，而且由於鄉鎮企業的快速發展，加速了勞動力向非農產業的轉移。於是，當年，東莞提出了「向農村工業化進軍」的奮鬥目標。

農村工業化推動了城鄉一體化和城市化進程。一九九二年，東莞確立「按現代化城市格局建設東莞」的發展戰略，使東莞很快就從原來的農村鄉鎮變為城鄉一體化的組團城市。從二○○一年開始，東莞掀起新一輪城市建設高潮。

就像中國很多發展中的城市一樣，城市與農村的視覺界限已不再那麼清晰，農村蓋起太多的小洋樓。最近幾年，城市人到農村旅游居住似乎變得流行起來，而在三十年前，他們想離開的恰恰也是農村。

受益於經濟快速發展，東莞在廣東率先實行免徵農業稅、普及高中階段教育、免除城鄉義務教育階段學生學雜費和書本費，在全國率先實行農（居）民養老保險、農（居）民基本醫療保險和計劃生育養老保險制度。

有人認為，這條路子，代表了中國農村走向城市化、實現現代化的方向。中共中央辦公廳調研室曾指出「東莞之路提供了我國城市化的一種現實可行的模式」，「對我國實現現代化會得到一些重要啟示」。

▎「東莞塞車，全球缺貨」

事情總是在不斷變化中，有些向好的方向發展。

即使在上世紀八○年代取得驚人的發展成績，但東莞人沒有躺在功勞簿上，而是不斷尋找新機會。那時候東莞基本上是勞動密集型產業，技術含量低，附加值低，主要依靠增加外地勞動力來支撐經濟增長，經濟發展形式粗放。

隨著越來越多的 IT 企業的不斷進入，並成群落。東莞經濟發生了深刻的變革。東莞的外貿出口總額從一九七八年的 0.39 億美元，增加到二○○七年的 602.32 億美元，增長 1543.4 倍，年均增長 27.7%。東莞成為繼深圳、上海之後全國出口額最高的城市，在各地級市中排名第一。

「東莞塞車，全球缺貨」，還曾有人這樣說「東莞塞車，世界感冒」，因為這裡的電腦主板、磁頭、驅動器的產量，占了全球的75%以上。「不論你在哪裡下單，都在東莞製造」。東莞成為現代製造業名城已是事實。

東莞需要也必須實現產業結構的轉型升級，向更高級的經濟發展方式轉變。一九九四年東莞對外宣布，東莞已基本實現了農村工業化，這是東莞「第一次工業革命」的結束，接下來要不失時機地推進「第二次工業革命」。

「第二次工業革命」被賦予的內涵是由勞動密集型工業向技術密集型工業邁進，使「數量型」經濟逐步向「質量型」經濟轉變。其被提出和實施，標誌著東莞經濟開始了升級轉型。

東莞抓住了難得的機遇，承接到了第二波的國際產業轉移。那時東莞的先進 IT 產業迅猛發展，東莞被人稱為「中國的 IT 之都」，並辦起了電博會，成為當時全球的四大國際電腦資訊博覽會之一。東莞是全球最大的電腦零部件生產製造基地，電腦百分之九十五的零配件在東莞都有生產。

　　三十多年的時間裡，從「三來一補」方式起步，東莞外向型經濟產業層次不斷提升，產品內涵不斷升級，進入八〇年代主要承接香港紡織、製鞋箱包、玩具等傳統製造業，企業規模小，產品附加值低；進入九〇年代，台灣及日韓地區電腦周邊產品為主的 IT 製造業大量進入東莞，令東莞成為製造之都。

　　當然不僅僅是 IT 製造業。東莞最後形成了門類齊全、配套完善、技術先進、涉及三十多個行業和六萬多種產品的製造業體系，世界 上大多數工業產品都可以在東莞企業群體的「工業生物鏈」中找到 其配套的行業和產品。在某種意義上，東莞是「MADE IN CHINA」的樣本區域，但凡任何有關製造業的風吹草動，總能在東莞找到分析樣本。東莞成了電子信息、電氣機械及設備、紡織服裝鞋帽、食品飲料、造紙及紙製品等各類製造業的「代工廠」。

　　東莞還是「鞋業之都」「服裝之都」和「玩具之都」。全球每十雙鞋中就有一雙屬於「東莞製造」。它還是「服裝之都」，在幾乎沒有季節交替感覺、十二月仍可以穿短袖衣、一根羊毛也不生產的東莞市大朗鎮，年銷售毛衣超過十億件，全球平均每五個人就有一人身著大朗生產的毛衣。

江門：
依舊海之門

「僑鄉」人傑地靈

我們吃過晚飯，熱氣已經退了。太陽落下了山坡，只留下一段燦爛的紅霞在天邊。

我們走過一段石子路，很快就到了河邊。在河邊大樹下，我們發現了幾隻小船。

我們陸續跳上一隻船。一個朋友解開了繩，拿起竹竿一撥，船緩緩地動了，向河中心移去。

河面很寬，白茫茫的水上沒有一點波浪。船平靜地在水面移動。三支槳有規律地在水裡劃，那聲音就像一支樂曲。

在一個地方，河面變窄了。一簇簇樹葉伸到水面上。樹葉真綠得可愛。那是許多株茂盛的榕樹，看不出主幹在什麼地方。

當我說許多株榕樹的時候，朋友們馬上糾正我的錯誤。一個朋友說那裡只有一株榕樹，另一個朋友說是兩株。我見過不少榕樹，這樣大的還是第一次看見。

我們的船漸漸逼近榕樹了。我有機會看清它的真面目，真是一株大樹，枝幹的數目不可計數。枝上又生根，有許多根直垂到地上，伸進泥土裡。一部分樹枝垂到水面，從遠處看，就像一株大樹臥在水面上。

榕樹正在茂盛的時期，好像把它的全部生命力展示給我們看。那麼多的綠葉，一簇堆在另一簇上面，不留一點兒縫隙。那翠綠的顏色，明亮地照耀著我們的眼睛，似乎每一片綠葉上都有一個新的生命在顫動。這美麗的南國的樹！

船在樹下泊了片刻。岸上很濕，我們沒有上去。朋友說這裡是「鳥的天堂」，有許多鳥在這樹上做巢，農民不許人去捉它們。我彷彿聽見幾隻鳥撲翅的聲音，等我注意去看，卻不見一隻鳥的影兒。只有無數的樹根立在地上，像許多根木樁。土地是濕的，大概漲潮的時候河水會沖上岸去。「鳥的天堂」裡沒有一隻鳥，我不禁這樣想。於是船開了，一個朋友撥著槳，船緩緩地移向河中心。

　　第二天，我們劃著船到一個朋友的家鄉去。那是個有山有塔的地方。從學校出發，我們又經過那「鳥的天堂」。

　　這一次是在早晨。陽光照耀在水面，在樹梢，一切都顯得更加光明了。我們又把船在樹下泊了片刻。

　　起初周圍是靜寂的。後來忽然起了一聲鳥叫。我們把手一拍，便看見一隻大鳥飛了起來。接著又看見第二隻，第三隻。我們繼續拍掌，樹上就變得熱鬧了，到處都是鳥聲，到處都是鳥影。大的，小的，花的，黑的，有的站在樹枝上叫，有的飛起來，有的在撲翅膀。

　　我注意地看著，眼睛應接不暇，看清楚了這只，又錯過了那只，看見了那隻，另一隻又飛起來了。一隻畫眉鳥飛了出來，被我們的掌聲一嚇，又飛進了葉叢，站在一根小枝上興奮地叫著，那歌聲真好聽。

　　當小船向著高塔下面的鄉村划去的時候，我回頭看那被拋在後面的茂盛的榕樹。我感到一點兒留戀。昨天是我的眼睛騙了我，那「鳥的天堂」的確是鳥的天堂啊！

——巴金《鳥的天堂》

一九三三年，中國近代最知名的作家之一巴金來到江門市新會區會城鎮天馬河的河心沙洲遊覽。島上有一株五百多年歷史的大榕樹，這棵樹的樹枝深垂到地上，扎入土中，成為新的樹幹，隨著時間的推移，這棵大榕樹竟獨木成林，林中棲息著成千上萬隻鳥雀，巴金有感而發，寫出了多次進入小學語文教材的散文——《鳥的天堂》，成為幾代中國人的精神記憶。

　　四十九年後的一九八二年，巴金又為這一景觀親筆題名「小鳥天堂」，自此，小鳥天堂名播天下。如今，這裡已經是全國最大的天然賞鳥樂園，亦是新會著名的國際級生態旅遊景點。

　　鳥的天堂，就像是江門這座城市特點的寫照，鳥兒忽來忽去，但終不會離沙洲而去。人亦如是。

　　江門地處西江與其支流蓬江匯合處，蓬江北面的蓬萊山與江南的煙墩山對峙似門，故名「江門」。

　　江門自古是人才輩出之地。「一門三院士，九子皆才俊」，出生於江門新會的近代著名思想家梁啟超九個子女，人人成才、各有所長。

　　梁啟超被公認是清末優秀的學者，中國歷史上一位百科全書式人物。在結束清王朝統治的辛亥革命前，他與革命派論戰中發明了一種新文體，介於古文與白話文之間，平易暢達、句法靈活，深受時人喜愛。梁啟超是中國第一個在文章中使用「中華民族」一詞的人。

　　他最為中國人所知的，還是在一八九五年與數千名舉人聯名上書清朝的光緒皇帝，反對在甲午戰爭中失敗後簽訂喪權辱國的《馬關條約》，是謂「公車上書」。隨後，他與自己的老師康有為在皇

帝的支持下發動戊戌變法，提倡科學文化，改革政治、教育制度，
發展農、工、商業。

一百多天後，變法失敗，絕大多數新政都被取消。但中國近代
第一所國立大學京師大學堂得以保留。一九一二年，京師大學堂更
名為北京大學。北京大學一直是中國最好的大學之一。

江門地處珠江三角洲西部。江門轄下的新會區（市）、開平
市、台山市、恩平市、鶴山市，由於五地人文風俗基本一致，故以
「五邑」著稱，聞名海內外。祖籍江門的華僑、華人和港澳台同胞
近四百萬，分佈在全世界五大洲一百零七個國家和地區，在亞洲地
區的約占百分之二十，美洲地區的約占百分之七十。

中國最著名的僑鄉有四個：江門、泉州、潮汕、梅州。泉州、
潮汕、梅州三個僑鄉的華僑大部分在東南亞，只有五邑的華僑主要
分佈在美國、加拿大和澳大利亞。這使得五邑僑鄉在保留中國傳統
文化的同時，還會積極推動中外文化交流，從建築、飲食、服飾到
風俗習慣，隨處可見中西交融的痕跡。

司徒美堂就是其中一位代表。

一八六八年四月三日，他出生在廣東開平縣赤崁鎮一個農民家
庭。一八八〇年三月，年僅十二歲的司徒美堂從開平步行至香港，
搭乘渡輪，隻身遠渡美國。

一八九四年，司徒美堂來到波士頓，成立了安良堂，打出了
「鋤強扶弱，除暴安良」的旗號，很快就成為洪門致公堂旗下的強
勢團體，最後發展到全美國三十一個城市都有安良堂，規模浩大，
成員達二萬多人。一九〇五年，司徒美堂在紐約成立了「安良總
堂」，當時的法律顧問是後來的美國總統——富蘭克林·羅斯福。

司徒美堂後與孫中山相識，孫中山在美活動期間，為保護孫中山的安全，他全程當貼身保鏢兼廚師。一九一一年四月，廣州黃花崗起義失敗後，同盟會急需十五萬美元救急，司徒美堂發動洪門致公堂的兄弟募捐。但他很清楚，這麼龐大的數額靠華僑募捐，斷難在短時間內湊齊。情急之下，他把在加拿大多倫多、溫哥華、維多利亞和金山大廈的四所致公堂大廈典押出去。後來又變賣幾座致公堂大樓，籌足了十五萬美元，支援了武裝起義。同年武昌起義後，孫中山由美歸國的旅費，也是司徒美堂等人提供。

一九三二年，「一‧二八」淞滬事變爆發，蔡廷鍇將軍率領十九路 軍將士英勇抵抗日寇。消息傳到美國，司徒美堂馬上組織募捐，帶 著捐款回到祖國慰問將士，他和蔡廷鍇也成了莫逆之交。

「僑」是江門的城市「DNA」，是江門區別於其他城市的根本之 處。二〇一五年開始，江門正式啟動「中國僑都」建設，提出擦亮「中 國僑都」的城市名片。江門市還出台實施了僑務強市規劃綱要及行 動方案。二〇一六年底，江門市提出，要大力發展全域旅遊、建設旅遊 強市，創建中國國際特色旅遊目的地，開平市、台山市被確定為國 家全域旅遊示範區創建單位。

發展僑務旅遊，中國僑都千里「潮人徑」成為重要抓手。「潮人徑」提倡用腳步去丈量城市的繁華，利用現有公路、村道、林道、登山小道、田園小路等線路，串聯自然保護區、風景名勝區、歷史古蹟、古村落、田園風光等景觀節點，形成具有僑鄉特色的城鄉慢行步行徑系統。二〇一七年，江門全市將建設總長達三千公里的「潮人徑」。在一段時間內，「潮人徑」最後爭取達到一萬公里，打造「廣東第一步行徑」。

百年碉樓和僑村

　　開平赤坎鎮一位姓關的老人有三十多位親戚在美國和加拿大生活。在僑鄉開平，像他這樣的家庭比比皆是。據說，開平有六十五萬人口，在海外的鄉親則有七十五萬之眾。

　　聞名遐邇的碉樓，就記載著一個個華僑家庭或家族的興衰，也維繫著源於當地並延伸到世界各地的鄉情和愛國傳統。從最初到北美挖金礦、修鐵路，到後來下南洋割膠開莊園，再到現在移居國外，碉樓見證了江門一代又一代人帶著夢想開拓、跋涉的故事。

　　五邑的僑鄉建築，完全融合了西方建築的特色，這其中，開平碉樓最為出名也最具特色。開平碉樓融合了中國傳統鄉村建築文化與西方建築文化的獨特建築藝術，成為中國華僑文化的紀念豐碑，體現了中國華僑與民眾主動接受西方文化的歷程。

　　開平碉樓的數量達到一千八百多座。二〇〇七年，「開平碉樓與村落」正式列入《世界遺產名錄》，成為中國第三十五處世界遺產，中國由此誕生了首個華僑文化的世界遺產項目。

　　世界遺產委員會這樣評價廣東開平碉樓：是村落中修建的一種具有防衛功能的多層塔樓式建築。這些碉樓與周圍的鄉村景觀和諧共存，體現了中西建築結構和裝飾形式複雜而絢麗的融合。

　　明朝以後，江門地區一度土匪猖獗，社會治安混亂。加上當地河流多，每遇颱風暴雨，洪澇災害頻發，聰明的江門人選擇在村中修建碉樓以求自保。

　　二十世紀二〇年代，碉樓迎來修建的高峰期。在海外辛苦了幾十年的華僑帶上積蓄回到家鄉，為了保護家人和財產安全，陸續建起以防盜功能為主的碉樓。

開平碉樓多是多層建築，遠高於一般的民居，便於居高臨下防禦；碉樓的牆體比普通的民居厚實堅固，不怕匪盜鑿牆或火攻；碉樓的窗戶比民居開口小，多有鐵柵和窗扇，外設鐵板窗門。碉樓上部的四角，一般都建有突出懸挑的全封閉或半封閉的角堡（俗稱「燕子窩」），角堡內開設了向前和向下的射擊孔，可以居高臨下地還擊進村之敵；同時，碉樓各層牆上開設有射擊孔，增加了樓內居民的攻擊點。

開平碉樓有不同的使用功能，也就有了不同的分類：眾樓、居樓和更樓。

眾樓建在村後，由全村人家或若干戶人家集資共同興建，每戶分房一間，為臨時躲避土匪或洪水使用。居樓也多建在村後，由富有人家獨資建造，它結合防衛和居住兩大功能，空間開敞，生活設施齊全。更樓主要建在村口或村外山岡、河岸，多配有探照燈和報警器，便於提前發現匪情，向各村預警。

開平碉樓的上部造型最具表現力，人們著力運用外國建築中的穹頂、山花、柱式等建築元素大做文章，形成了千樓千面的建築式樣。不同的建築造型反映著樓主人的經濟實力、審美情趣和受外來建築文化影響的程度。

位於開平市塘口鎮的自力村碉樓群是世界文化遺產地之一，因中國電影《讓子彈飛》在此拍攝而名聲大噪。《讓子彈飛》是二〇一〇年上映的一部電影，講述了北洋年間，南部中國一場驚天動地的火車劫案之後，號令山林的綠林悍匪張牧之，遭遇行走江湖的通天大騙老湯，兩人從生死宿敵變成莫逆之交，然而真正的決戰才剛剛開始，南國一霸黃四郎虎視眈眈鎮守鵝城，一場場驚心動魄的決鬥連環上演。

二〇一七年，中國電影院的銀幕總數已經超過四萬塊，成為世界上電影銀幕最多的國家。中國電影似乎迎來了最好的時代，但真正深入人心的好電影卻變得稀少。《讓子彈飛》被認為是這個時代值得記錄的電影之一。

《讓子彈飛》的導演是姜文，同時也是主演。這是他的第四部電影，他是當代中國電影界的最重要人物之一。

雲幻樓是自力村十五座碉樓之一。一九二一年，占地面積八十平方米的雲幻樓建成。

這一年，中國仍在尋求獨立富強之路。對中國人來說，這年最為重要的是中國共產黨第一次全國代表大會在上海舉行，中國共產黨誕生。二十八年後，中國共產黨成為中國的執政黨，建立中華人民共和國。

雲幻樓的建設者方文嫻曾旅居馬來西亞，熱心公益。一九一八年，方文嫻自捐五千元、募捐一點七萬元回鄉興辦強亞學校。日本侵華期間，他曾捐巨資支持抗日及購買自由公債。

為在家鄉落葉歸根，他建了這座碉樓。五層高的雲幻樓，外部造型和裝飾帶有明顯的西式風格。但在樓內，還保存著方文嫻及家人使用過的生活用具，一派中國南方農村家居的傳統形象。

他還親自撰寫樓聯：雲龍風虎際會常懷怎奈壯志莫愁只贏得湖海生涯空山歲月　幻影曇花身世如夢何妨豪情自放無負此陽春煙景大塊文章。

對聯表達的是：自己常有大幹一番事業的願望，可惜壯志難以實現，只能漂泊江湖，無奈蹉跎歲月；儘管一切皆是幻影，還是要抒發豪情，不能辜負了眼下如煙的春色、錦繡的文章。

在中國文化中，對聯要有橫批，這副對聯的橫批是：只談風月。這位商人把自己愛國、愛鄉的豪情壯志，及對動盪年代的憤懣和苦悶展示在對聯中。

不僅僅是碉樓，在開平的鄉間，就有一些村子，連村名也深深被打上了「僑」的印記，這些村子的出現和建設，就是一部縮影版的僑鄉移民歷史，其背後書寫著僑鄉人民艱苦奮鬥的創業精神，以及對故國情深的愛國情懷。

提起僑村的建築，讓人感慨的是建造者在選材方面的講究，奢華的房屋建造所需要的材料，有些是從海外直接採購。「加拿大村」僱請加拿大的設計師結合中西文化元素規劃設計而成，並將村莊、別墅建設圖紙從海外帶回家鄉依圖而建。而建造別墅的鋼筋、水泥和木頭，也是加拿大華僑從加拿大運到香港，再由香港運回開平，來回一次需三個多月。

走進「緬甸村」，十二間兩層高的大屋分兩行排列，整齊坐落在田野當中，而在村子前面則是空曠的地面，外面便是水塘。房子與房子之間的距離都是「等距離」，大概有二米寬，樓頂為硬山頂式瓦面結構，牆體為青磚結構，樓梯、樓閣大門均為柚木結構，橫梁為「工」字鐵外加柚木。

這些房子大部分是兩房兩廊一廳，小部分為一房一廊，而建房所需的柚木，從緬甸購進，而水泥、鋼鐵等，則從香港等地僱船運回。「緬甸村」的建設者是許遂興，為了生計，他帶著弟弟許純興遠走他鄉到緬甸，並在一家木材廠做起了雜工，因為勤奮努力，幾年後，他們有了一定的積蓄，並辦了一個名叫「萬興隆」的木板廠。鼎盛時，經營的店鋪多達幾十間，成為當地有名的商人。盡管在緬甸日子過得十分滋潤，但許家兩兄弟還是免不了對家鄉的思念，於是他們後來回到家鄉建房。

海外「發芽」根在江門

「爸爸去金山，快快要寄銀，全家靠住你，有銀好寄回。」這是首籍江門的華僑們熟悉的民謠。在舊中國，大量中國人被迫「賣豬仔」，漂洋過海到美國舊金山洗礦砂、做苦力，參與建造美國中央太平洋大鐵路。建築鐵路的華工百分之八十是江門人。太多人長眠在異國他鄉。

一篇名為《濃濃僑情滿江門》的文章介紹，孫中山領導辛亥革命，組建「興中會」「同盟會」和國民黨時，江門華僑都踴躍參加。孫中山組織了十次武裝起義，所需經費多靠華僑支持，其中江門華僑貢獻最大。他曾說「華僑為革命之母」，表明了海外華僑對革命極大的貢獻。

一九三七年至一九四五年八月，江門華僑在美國捐款就達五千六百萬美元以上。當時國民政府共發行六期救國公債，總額達三十億元，其中僅江門華僑就認購了十一點一億元。

二〇一〇年全面對外開放的江門五邑華僑華人博物館，館藏的四萬餘件華僑實物，全面忠實地記錄了這段歷史，展現五邑籍華僑華人在海外的艱辛創業以及回報家鄉的感人故事。

台山斗山鎮六村美唐村人陳宜禧，一八四四年生，十一歲時赴美，後來參加美國鐵路建設，成為鐵路工程師。再後經商，經營「廣德號」，參與了許多西雅圖的承建工程，成為有影響的華商。美國排華期間，陳宜禧不畏強暴，為維護華人權益積極奔走，團結組織同胞奮勇抗爭，受到僑胞的欽佩和愛戴，成為頗具影響力的僑領。

六十歲時，陳宜禧放棄在美國優越的生活條件，回到貧困的家鄉，帶領鄉親集資建造一條屬於中國人的鐵路——新寧鐵路。新寧鐵路非但不借洋款，不收洋股，且不借洋工，自行修築，從籌備、設計、修建、經營到管理都是由中國人獨力完成，開風氣之先。他決心要「以中國人之資本，築中國人之鐵路；以中國人之力量，創中國史之奇功！」

新寧鐵路從一九〇六年五月一日正式動工到一九二〇年三月三十日竣工，歷時十四年。鐵路全長一百三十三公里，共有車站四十六個，橋樑二百一五座，涵洞二百三十六個，並先後建成公益碼頭、北街碼頭、公益機器廠、牛灣船務等一大批工程，「轉車盤」和輪渡火車更是中國鐵路史上的創舉，確立了以台城為交通樞紐、以新寧鐵路為幹線的水陸交通網絡，成為民國時期江門五邑社會經濟發展的大動脈。

一九三三年，巴金乘坐新寧鐵路火車輪渡過潭江，寫下了著名的散文《機器的詩》。

文中寫道：「為了去看一個朋友，我做了一次新寧鐵路上的旅客。我和三個朋友一路從會城到公益，我們坐在火車上大約坐三個鐘頭。時間長，天氣熱，但是我並不覺得寂寞。

南國的風物的確有一種迷人的力量。在我的眼裡一切都顯出一種夢境般的美：那樣茂盛的綠樹，那樣明亮的紅土，那一塊一塊的稻田，那一堆一堆的房屋，還有明鏡似的河水，高聳的碉樓。南國的鄉村，雖然裡面包含了不少的痛苦，但是表面上它們還是很平靜，很美麗!到了潭江，火車停下來。車輪沒有動，外面的景物卻開始慢慢地移動了。這不是什麼奇蹟，這是新寧鐵路上的一段最美麗的工程。」

新寧鐵路前後經營三十多年，抗戰期間，遭到日軍嚴重破壞，後被國民政府下令拆除，現僅存北街火車站舊址。

數據顯示，祖籍江門的華僑、華人和港澳台同胞近四百萬人，遍布全球一百零七個國家和地區，華僑、華人與市內人口基本相當，擁有「海內外兩個江門」的說法。

美國原駐華大使駱家輝、美國舊金山市長李孟賢、美國奧克蘭市長關麗珍、澳門特別行政區行政長官崔世安等政界人物，劉德華、周潤發、譚詠麟、梁朝偉、甄子丹等香港演藝明星的祖籍都是江門。

華僑愛國愛鄉，通過捐助公益、投資興業等方式幫助家鄉發展。截至二〇一五年底，為家鄉捐資捐物達七十二點六億港元，回鄉投資累計達二百零一點二億美元。江門特別設立「榮譽市民」授榮制度，以表彰在促進江門社會文明發展慈善公益事業、對外友好交往、經濟科技建設等方面做出突出貢獻的海外僑胞、外籍人士和國內人士。自一九九三年以來，先後共授予八批七百位海內外人士「江門市榮譽市民」稱號。

黃小娟就是「江門市榮譽市民」，她在馬來西亞沙巴州長大，早年在加拿大求學。大學畢業後，跟隨父親做房地產生意，一步步成為沙巴著名的女企業家。

黃小娟的父親黃國先後捐資百餘萬元，為台山當地學校修建操場、改造舊教學樓。黃小娟記得，一九八〇年開始，父親每年都要回老家探親。一九九八年，首次到台山的黃小娟聽說有小學需修繕，立即發動捐款。

對黃小娟來說，能成為江門和馬來西亞沙巴兩城之間經貿、文化往來的橋樑感到榮耀，對江門自己也有一種責任感。

祖籍江門的海外華人佼佼者中，應該還包括方美梅。一九九四年第三十六屆格萊美音樂獎上，方美梅憑藉《十個召喚者的故事》獲得最佳音樂製作獎。這是華人第一次站在格萊美獎的領獎台上。

一九六四年出生於美國三藩市的方美梅，是第二代華人，祖籍廣東省開平市塘口鎮強亞村委會上塘村。她的父親方創傑是當地著名的僑領，早在二十世紀五〇年代已在三藩市創辦了以自己名字命名的保險行。大學期間，方美梅就嘗試影視製作，畢業後製作音樂錄影片。

為了表彰方美梅所取得的成績，三藩市市長辦公室於一九九四年七月十六日除了頒獎表揚方美梅外，還宣布十六日為「方美梅日」。

昌明文庫・悅讀中國　A0607034

中國夢・廣東故事——活力的廣東

作　　者　徐　靜

版權策畫　李煥芹

責任編輯　呂玉姍

發 行 人　陳滿銘

總 經 理　梁錦興

總 編 輯　陳滿銘

副總編輯　張晏瑞

編 輯 所　萬卷樓圖書股份有限公司

排　　版　菩薩蠻數位文化有限公司

印　　刷　百通科技股份有限公司

封面設計　菩薩蠻數位文化有限公司

出　　版　昌明文化有限公司

桃園市龜山區中原街 32 號

電話 (02)23216565

發　　行　萬卷樓圖書股份有限公司

臺北市羅斯福路二段 41 號 6 樓之 3

電話 (02)23216565

傳真 (02)23218698

電郵 SERVICE@WANJUAN.COM.TW

大陸經銷

廈門外圖臺灣書店有限公司

電郵 JKB188@188.COM

ISBN 978-986-496-398-0

2019 年 3 月初版

定價：新臺幣 300 元

如何購買本書：

1. 轉帳購書，請透過以下帳戶

合作金庫銀行　古亭分行

戶名：萬卷樓圖書股份有限公司

帳號：0877717092596

2. 網路購書，請透過萬卷樓網站

網址 WWW.WANJUAN.COM.TW

大量購書，請直接聯繫我們，將有專人為您

服務。客服：(02)23216565 分機 610

如有缺頁、破損或裝訂錯誤，請寄回更換

國家圖書館出版品預行編目資料

中國夢.廣東故事 ——活力的廣東 / 徐靜著.
-- 初版. -- 桃園市：昌明文化出版；臺北
市：萬卷樓發行, 2019.03

　冊；　公分

ISBN 978-986-496-398-0(平裝)

1.區域研究 2.廣東省

673.3　　　　　　　　108002848